# FULL PARDON

# Full Pardon

BILLY McFETRIDGE
WITH MICHAEL APICHELLA

KINGSWAY PUBLICATIONS
EASTBOURNE

*Front cover photos: Frank Spooner Pictures Ltd*

**British Library Cataloguing in Publication Data**
McFetridge, Bill
    Full pardon.
    I. Title   II. Apichella, Michael
    248.146

ISBN 0860659763

Printed in Great Britain for
KINGSWAY PUBLICATIONS LTD
1 St Anne's Road, Eastbourne, E Sussex BN21 3UN by
Clays Ltd, St. Ives plc
Typeset by J&L Composition Ltd, Filey, North Yorkshire

This book is affectionately dedicated to my mother
in gratitude for her many tender mercies
shown to me over the years; and to my
fellow prisoners, wherever they may be found

# Foreword

Good news from Northern Ireland! God is able to change the hardest hearts. He can heal the deepest prejudice which leads to violence and death.

*Full Pardon* is a story that will give hope to the great army of ordinary Christian people who are working for a better day in our strife-torn land. 'What is the answer to Ulster's problems?' is a question often asked. Billy McFetridge replies: 'I don't know the answer but I believe that Christ will be the solution as he has been in my life and in the lives of many former terrorists, Protestant as well as Catholic.'

Charged with fifty-eight offences in a frightening catalogue of crimes, Billy faced a bleak future. In prison he found freedom in Christ. His life was completely turned around and now he is working full-time with Prison Fellowship, a Christian association dedicated to helping prisoners and their families.

Behind Billy's remarkable conversion stands the wonderful witness of a small band of faithful Christians who cared and shared and prayed; dedicated chaplains like Bill Vance and Jim Hughes, and prison visitors Agnes Hancock, James McIlroy and others from Prison Fellowship. And behind them a great company of praying people who know they can reach into every prison cell in Ireland and by faith reclaim for Christ those who are dominated by the powers of evil.

It is my fervent wish that this book will be widely read. I might suggest that Christian people would not only read it but use their influence to see that it reaches thousands of young people in schools and youth clubs.

Cecil Kerr
**Director of the Christian Renewal Centre, Rostrevor**

# Introduction

At long last, the day I had prayed and dreamed about finally arrived. The prison officer opened the large gate, turned to me and said, 'Away you go.' Before I knew what was happening, I was a free man standing out in the car park of the Maze Prison. My family rushed forward to greet me. Once again, I was a member of society.

A few months later, I was enrolled as a student at Belfast Bible College where I was preparing for a career as a prison evangelist. Through college contacts, I was invited to speak in Belfast. People in church and civic groups were asking me to explain how I went from packing a 9mm pistol to an RSV Bible.

In time, I began to crisscross the country, north and south of the border, telling my story of God's amazing grace—in my life and in the lives of other terrorists whom I'd met behind bars. One person after another said to me, 'Why don't you write a book about your conversion?' My usual reply was, 'Me? I can hardly write a letter, never mind a book!' But as time moved on, the question of writing a book became more prominent in my mind.

One day I met and spent time talking to Harry

Lee. Harry is Chinese, and he himself was a prisoner during the Cultural Revolution in his homeland. He was tortured for his beliefs. After I had told him my story, he smiled and said, 'Billy, we each have a story to tell, and God wants us to tell those stories.'

The 'seed' of this book you are now reading was sown in the office of Mrs Anthea Harrison, one of my lecturers at Belfast Bible College. Anthea suggested that she would interview me on tape. The result was a synopsis of my life which we sent to a publisher. To our surprise and delight, Tony Collins of Kingsway Publications wrote back saying, 'Yes, we are very interested in your story.'

Many books have been written since the 'troubles' began some twenty-two years ago. I have read quite a few of them. Unfortunately, many of these stories seem to glorify the violence which has become almost an everyday occurrence in our troubled land. Hence, I have specifically tried to play down the violence in this book.

As I travel around meeting different people in churches, especially if I go outside of Northern Ireland, I am asked the same question: 'What is the answer to Ulster's problems?' I don't know the answer. But I do know that a solution will be found. I believe that Christ will be the solution as he's been in my life and in the lives of many former terrorists, Protestant as well as Catholic. That's the message of this book.

I'd like to thank my wife, Martha, for her love and support at all times, my church which helped to pray this book into being, and, of course, my co-author, Michael Apichella, for the many hours he spent on the manuscript, and for his unending support throughout the writing of this book.

I would also like to thank my friends and colleagues at Prison Fellowship: Frank, Robin, Patricia, Michelle and Peter. Thanks to my good friends Agnes Hancock who has now gone to glory, James McIlroy, Ron, Maureen, Bernie, Anthea, Iris, Cal, Big Roy, Packie, Bobby, Paul, Carol, Joe, Eddie, Liam and Marie; the prison chaplains; my sister Betty; my former wife, Christine and my son Christopher, as well as the many, many others who are not mentioned here by name.

I want to point out that a percentage of the book's royalties will be given to the Larne YMCA, a worthwhile cause which is very close to my heart.

Finally, many of the names in this book have been changed in order to protect the innocent.

# Chapter One

The abrasive trill of the telephone filled our tiny council flat just as I switched on the television to watch *Dad's Army*. 'Now who would that be?' said my mother. I stood up and took the call. 'Is Billy there?' Automatically, I turned my back on Mum. 'Speaking.'

'Tonight's the night, Billy. Be in the pub in fifteen minutes.'

'What's the job?' I asked.

'You'll be told when you get there. Don't be late.'

I put the receiver down and walked into my bedroom, shutting the door. With a soft grunt, I dropped onto my knees at the foot of the bed and probed under the mattress. A smile of satisfaction spread across my face as my eager fingers found what they were looking for: a Browning 9mm pistol and a full clip of cartridges. Loading the gun, I pressed the safety catch in place and stood. I tucked the gun into my belt, grabbed a jacket and walked to the front door of the flat. 'I'm going out, Mum.'

At the pub, I stood waiting with my elbow hooked

easily on the rim of the wooden bar, a pint of Double Diamond in one hand, a Marlboro in the other. Time turtled by. Eventually, a man nursing a pint of Guinness sidled up next to me and nodded. 'Evening, Billy,' he said. The adrenalin began pumping in my veins and my heart rate increased. 'Evening,' I replied calmly.

'The name's Mike. Got everything?' he asked.

I nodded as I patted a small bulge beneath my jacket.

'Let's go over to the football club. There's a mate of mine who's going to help us with our little job tonight. He's called Ian.'

We polished off our drinks and walked out into the darkness.

As the last of the members of Larne's Football Club spilled out into the chilly night, the three of us crept to the side of the building and hid in the shadows. Mike carelessly bumped into a rubbish bin sending the lid clattering onto the pavement. We froze, ready to make a dash if need be. After a few minutes, it became clear that nobody had heard the noise. Slowly, we relaxed and waited.

I knew this was going to be a straightforward assignment: we would wait until the last of the customers had left the premises, and then we would force our way inside, stealing the club's money to buy more guns for the Ulster Defence Association to which we three belonged. These guns would ensure that Ulster remained Protestant and British. It didn't concern us that the football club we were about to rob was a Protestant establishment. The end justified the means. For terrorists, it always does.

The men inside were taking a long time to disperse. I could feel my companions becoming more impatient with each minute that ticked by. As the bells of Larne chimed eleven times, a set of headlights sped into the car park sending up a spray of gravel. Squinting into the bright lights, I felt a sharp pang in the pit of my stomach. It was a police car. The men inside the club must have heard the noise and, becoming suspicious, called the cops. The passenger-side officer thrust open the car door and called calmly, 'All right, come on out.' The policeman at the wheel laughed. They must have thought we were a harmless couple doing our courting in the dark. My eyes flashed from my mates back to the police car.

'Do you hear me? Come on out!' called the cop. None of us dared speak.

Before the officer could switch on his torch, Ian drew his .32 revolver and unlocked the safety catch. Next, he raced past the policeman. Instinctively, I pulled my balaclava down over my face but remained rooted to the spot.

The driver leapt out of the car and commanded, 'Stop, you!' I noticed neither of the policemen had drawn his revolver. 'Stop, I said!' Ian skidded to a halt, pivoted and, crouching, he took aim. There followed a loud blast. The impact of the slug punched the cop to the gravel where he lay gasping in a spreading pool of dark blood. The other policeman rushed over to his stricken partner. Turning, Ian sprinted across the darkened football pitch.

Two men came rushing out of the football club. 'What's going on out here?' the bartender called to the police.

'Get back!' retorted the cop. 'He's been shot!'

Taking advantage of this diversion, Mike bolted, sending the gravel flying into the air.

My heart pounded against my rib cage. Now I was alone. Any moment other police cars would arrive on the scene and it would all be over for me. It was now or never. Drawing my weapon, I stepped out of the shadows, unlocking the safety catch. Holding the Browning 9mm in both hands, I snarled at the officer, 'Move and you're dead!'

'Don't shoot,' he pleaded.

'Now lie face down next to your friend there. Move!'

I could see that this was a young officer, maybe twenty or so. He was trembling as he obeyed my command. Keeping my gun trained on the officer's head, I eased past the two men. I then lifted my knees and charged off in the same direction as Mike whom I could see waiting for me at the edge of the car park. The whole episode was over in seconds.

'That was too close for comfort,' I said between puffs. I thrust my gun into Mike's hands and said, 'Stash this.' Then we trotted off in opposite directions.

Once in town, I stopped in an alleyway, then took off my balaclava and brushed my hair with my fingers. *Calm down and act naturally*, I thought. Leaning against a door frame until I caught my breath, I decided to stop in a club for a drink before going home.

Standing at the crowded bar and sipping a whisky and water, I frowned at my reflection in the mirror. The way Ian had panicked and pulled the trigger so freely made me furious. Admittedly, it was a tight spot, but had he waited, we probably could have bluffed our way out of the situation. Now, not only had we no money to show for our night's work, but we had a dead policeman on our hands as well.

Gradually the atmosphere of the club became oppressive; I decided to go down to the harbour to get some fresh air.

There was no relief at the quayside for me. The night was murky and depressing. You couldn't even see the bright lights of the Ballylumford power plant through the thick sea mist. 'Home me,' I said aloud, turning on my heel.

There was lots of traffic that night. Each time a car approached, I expected a cop to jump out and shout, 'Freeze.' At last, there were the council flats on the edge of Larne. Once inside, my mother asked, 'Have you heard about the shooting tonight?' She looked pale and drawn. I shook my head. 'Some poor young policeman's been shot at the football club.'

'Was he killed?'

'No. Just wounded.'

I smiled weakly and turned away. 'G'night, Mum. Got a long day tomorrow.' I closed the bedroom door behind me.

Feeling too exhausted to undress, I stretched my full six-foot frame across my bed and fished a packet of Marlboros from my breast pocket. A siren wailed far below my window somewhere in the streets of Larne. Lighting up, I sucked gratefully on that first puff, holding it in my lungs for as long as possible. Exhaling, I began to wonder when my luck would run out. Over the years, so many of my mates had been nicked or killed in the line of duty that I had lost count. Was all this worth it? Taking another long pull on the cigarette, I thought about why I'd joined the UDA in the first place. My mind went back over the years. Suddenly it was 23rd August 1972 and one of my father's cousins had been murdered by the IRA in Belfast.

# Chapter Two

To me, the headlines of the 23rd August 1972 Belfast *Newsletter* seemed to shriek out the news of Dad's cousin: 'James Frederick Johnston Murder Victim.' It was a brutal, execution-style murder—the sort in which the IRA specialised. Why Jim had been singled out for murder, and how it happened, is hard to say exactly for there were no witnesses. But according to the police investigation, it may have happened like this: James Frederick Johnston walked along the Grosvenor Road in Roman Catholic West Belfast. He didn't live in this part of the city; he only passed through on his way to work. Although the people there didn't know his name, they knew he was a Protestant for it's said in Belfast that the very cut of a man's clothes and the way he walks may tell others if he's Protestant or Catholic.

According to Jim's family, four days earlier he'd been approached by some Republican watchdogs after they'd found out he belonged to an organisation called LAW (the Loyalist Association of Workers). As Republicans, they were adamant that

19

he should find a new way to get to work. The message was clear: Loyalists stay out of the Grosvenor Road. Jim knew they were serious, so nobody knows why he risked going into Republican territory again. He might have been pressed for time and decided to risk it just once more. Maybe he wanted to show the IRA that Ulster is a free land and he could walk where he pleased. Only he knew his reasons for disobeying a clear warning.

Apparently, without further warning, four men grabbed Jim, twisting his arms behind his back. He was bundled into the back of a waiting van where they peeled off his shirt and vest. A sack was thrust over his head and his wrists and ankles were bound so tightly with twine that his skin was scraped raw. The van pulled away from the kerb and the men drove on in silence until they had left Belfast far behind. 'Stop here, Danny!' cried their leader.

'Where've you taken me? What's going on? Answer me!'

'You've been warned, Johnston. This is what we do to anyone who defies us,' he said, nodding to his mate. An unseen fist crashed into Jim's solar plexus. He gasped and bent double. Holding Jim's head down firmly between his knees, the leader ordered, 'Give him a back massage.' A short man with a sly smile began to run the steel barrel of a .32 revolver up and down Johnston's spine until his backbone was bruised and bleeding. 'OK, OK,' pleaded Jim, 'you've convinced me. I'll never cross you again. I'll find some other route to work. I swear to you.'

'A bit too late for that. Take the bag off his head.' Jim's eyes ran with tears. 'What're you going to do to me?' The four men passed around a packet of cigarettes and lit up. First they laughed at Jim and blew jets of smoke into his face. When he smiled back, the short one removed his cigarette and stubbed it out on Jim's cheek. Jim cringed in horror, but there wasn't room enough to move away. Next the three others removed their cigarettes and did the same until the back of the van smelled of burned flesh. Jim panted, and cursed. 'You won't get away with this. I'll get even with you bastards. You wait.'

'There's where you're wrong, Johnston. Dead wrong.' The back of the van was thrust open, and their victim was tumbled head over heels into a patch of high grass and weeds. Seconds later, all four men had drawn revolvers and they opened fire on Jim, who squirmed and dodged amid the popping, trying to roll away from the hail of bullets until his body went limp.

'That's enough,' said the leader. 'He's dead. Put him in the van and let's go back and leave him where we found him.'

The next day, two policemen conducting a routine investigation of an abandoned van in Belfast's Turin Street, discovered Jim's body. There were six holes in his skull as well as burns and lacerations on his face and wrists. After identification was confirmed, the police released the body to the morgue.

My family only learned of the murder the next day when I saw it in the morning paper. All of us were confused and appalled. Shortly after, a call from another family member confirmed the bad news of Jim's abduction and death. The police knew this was more than a straightforward homicide. It was a political statement, and our family had become embroiled in a war not of our making.

At the time of Jim's murder, I was in Larne on

leave from Germany where I was stationed in the army. Because the situation in Northern Ireland was so dicey in those days, our officers suggested that we soldiers living in Northern Ireland stay away from Ulster, or that we visit relatives in other parts of the United Kingdom, while on leave. But as far as I was concerned, the troubles at home had nothing to do with me, and in 1972 I hadn't an enemy in the world. During that leave, however, the troubles really came home to me because, for the first time, I had been directly affected by the violence. What had happened to Jim could just as easily have happened to my dad or to me.

The police rang us with the news of Jim's murder on the morning I was getting ready to return to Germany and while my father was working over the border as a long-distance lorry driver. As I've indicated, the police suspected the Provos as the perpetrators of the crime. I found myself in a jam: I was due back in Germany, but I knew I couldn't leave in the midst of our family's shock and grief. I rang through to local headquarters requesting permission to delay my return an extra few days in order to attend Jim's funeral. A gruff voice on the other end of the line ordered me to forget about the funeral and to return directly to Germany. 'Above all, McFetridge, you mustn't go to the funeral. A British soldier's presence at such an event might stir up more trouble. I'm sure you understand.'

But I stuck my heels in. 'Sir,' I retorted, 'if I'm not granted an official extension of my leave, I'll take an unofficial one.'

'Are you threatening me, McFetridge?' came the terse reply.

'Sir, a member of my family has been gunned

down in Belfast. What would you do if it was your family?'

In the end, I was given another seven days' leave, and, of course, I went to the funeral.

When someone you know is murdered, you naturally assume that the police will solve the case; that the murderers will be brought to justice. But it turned out that the murderers weren't going to be found and punished. The Ulster police's hands were tied by miles of official red tape which stretched all the way back to Whitehall. At the time, Belfast was a political gunpowder keg. The official policy was to keep things quiet and calm—at all costs. Jim's death was to be classified as one of the dozens of unfortunate statistics stemming from the troubles. There would be no attempt to find and charge the gunmen. When I realised this, I thought, *Can't someone do something about it? How long will the Provos be allowed to get away with murder?* Many of our neighbours in Larne were asking the same questions. To us, the British army was nothing but a paper tiger.

In the light of this, I concluded the Northern Irish people themselves must take up arms and fight for their rights. Maybe I could do something to put right the grim situation. As it happened, I could do nothing at the time as I was due back in Germany for the last few months before I demobbed.

The funeral was a blur to me. I hardly spoke to anyone, and when I did, I can't recall what I said. I was busy counting the seconds until I could get back to a country where nobody cares whether a man crosses himself and kneels or whether he just bows his head in church.

After my return to Germany, I forgot about the

injustice in Ulster. I was glad to be away from its troubles and pessimism. But the memory of poor Jim's death played on my mind, and Jim's case wasn't a one-off; others whom I knew well were getting killed too.

One incident which still grieves me happened to an army friend of mine called Tom. After being posted back to Northern Ireland, Tom bought a car from a man who was in the RUC (Royal Ulster Constabulary). Unbeknown to the constable, he had been under surveillance by the IRA and his car's registration number had been listed as a target for bombing. Meanwhile, Tom had bought the car. Since the IRA's intelligence noted only the car's registration and not the owner's name, my friend was literally driving around in a time bomb.

One night in Enniskillen, Tom and two companions had gone into a pub leaving the car parked in a side street. Apparently a member of the Provos had spotted the car's registration number and immediately set about wiring it with explosives.

Later that night, the three came out of the pub singing and laughing. They were still singing as Tom inserted his key in the starter. Mercifully they never knew what had hit them. All three lads were blown to pieces when the ignition was switched on.

Tom had been a conscientious and fun-loving young man, liked by all. He had no quarrel with anyone and only wanted to get on with his life. In a single turn of a key, his life and those of his companions were snuffed out. To be sure, similar identification mistakes had been made by the UDA as well. The point is, the troubles continued to haunt my life—even after I'd demobbed in 1973.

Around this time, I had trouble holding down a

steady job. I worked as a docker at Larne Harbour. I worked in a factory. The truth is, manual labour left much to be desired for me, so I would skive off and hang around in the pubs in Larne when I should have been at work.

One day I came in from the pub and my mother told me a friend of mine had rung and asked if I would ring him back. 'A friend?' I queried. 'Did he say who he was?'

'No, he just left this number.' Mum handed me a slip of paper. Puzzled, I picked up the telephone and dialled the strange number.

'Hello?'

'This is Billy McFetridge. I was told you rang me earlier.'

'Yes, that's right. My name's Ian. Can you chat?'

'Sure, what did you have in mind?'

'Well, I'll get right to the point, Billy. I know what happened to Jim Johnston, and I don't care much for the way the police have dragged their feet on the case. The fact is, Billy, Jim's not the only unsolved Protestant murder case in recent times, if you get what I mean.'

'Tell me about it,' I replied tacitly. 'So what do you want with me?'

'I . . . er, that is, we, me and a number of other lads from Larne, would like to invite you to join us in defending our rights against . . .' He paused. 'Against the Provos.'

'Are you with the UDA?'

'That's right.'

'But why me? I've been away from Northern Ireland for years. I'm out of touch.'

'Look, Billy, I'll put it to you like this. You're a trained soldier. You could be a great asset to us, and

25

I don't doubt you'd be promoted quickly to captain.' He could sense I was hesitant. 'But here I am puttin' the pressure on you, when really all I wanted to do was put the idea to you. Are you willin' to help us help Northern Ireland?'

As he spoke, I felt a surge of panic. I wanted to put the phone down and re-enlist in the army so I could get away from Ulster and its problems. After a long pause, I replied, 'I need time, man. Let me think about it. I'll keep this number and get back in touch with you in a few days, all right?'

'Yeah, sure, Billy. No pressure, lad. G'night.'

I put the phone down and swore out loud.

# Chapter Three

That telephone call proved to be the turning point in my life, for had it never been made, I might never have joined the ranks of the UDA or any other paramilitary group. Most likely, I'd have carried on working at odd jobs, and then gone abroad. But now the challenge was put directly to me: would I help to defend Ulster or would I bolt?

It was true that the military life was second nature to me. My father had been in the army for twenty years, and I had been in the army cadets around the time I joined the Forces myself. What's more, at the time, I was still in top physical condition. In the light of all this, I suppose I appeared to be a valuable asset to the paramilitaries. But the truth is I'd never been a committed soldier—not even on the day I enlisted in the army. The only reason I'd joined up was to get away from home.

It was a hot August, 1967. I was seventeen years old and had been in Belfast waiting for the train to Larne when I walked into an army careers office and said I wanted to join up. Of course, the recruiter nearly fell over as he clambered out of his chair and whisked me upstairs where a doctor waited to give me my medical. A few hours later, I was all but signed up. All that remained was my father's signature owing to my being under age. I was scared that I would be in trouble for doing such a daft thing as enlisting; scared that I'd have to go back to the careers officer and tell him that I couldn't be a soldier because my parents wouldn't let me. At age seventeen, this would be too humiliating for words. But my fears were unfounded. Dad signed the form straightaway and the very next night I was on a boat on my way to England for basic training in Yorkshire. I was full of a sense of joy and adventure.

The joy was to be short lived, but the adventure was about to begin.

The day I arrived at Catterick, I was taken to an open square where the physical training instructor presided. Everywhere panting young men were trotting around, jumping over benches, climbing up long ropes which stretched into infinity, or so it seemed to me as I stood there scowling.

Suddenly a spiteful voice commanded, 'Oi, you there. Up you go.' It was the PTI. He proffered a heavy rope and gave it an impatient shake. 'Come on, I 'aven't got all day. Upsy daisy, sonny.'

To me, the training centre appeared like some physical fitness nightmare. I didn't have to pinch myself to see if I was dreaming. It was real, all right. My army career might have ended right there, for the simple reason that I was terrified by the physical tortures which the PTI had assembled in that square. The sight of an authoritarian instructor and all those beefy young men going through their paces so confidently brought back the galling memories of my failed school days; the one thing I was most desperate to put behind me by joining up.

Part of why I failed, both in the classroom and in the school playground, was due to my acute shortsightedness. To my eyes, everything the teacher wrote on the blackboard was swimming about and blurred. My way of dealing with this was to act cool and uncommunicative. Perhaps I felt that this way I would never be called upon in class. On the playing field, my weak vision made me unco-ordinated and awkward. I survived there by staying off to the side when the teams were playing. This caused friction between me and the games master, but it preserved my dignity before my mates.

For a while this seemed to work, but one day a note was sent home from one of my teachers to my parents suggesting that I have my eyes tested. She suspected I needed glasses.

I was duly taken to a shop in Larne and there my teacher's guess was confirmed. I was fitted with a big, ugly pair of black National Health spectacles with lenses as thick as glass paperweights. For the first time in years, I could see clearly the world about me, but I hated the glasses. Tall, skinny and clumsy to start with, this new addition made me feel and look a right wally. I threatened not to wear them at school, but my father, with the aid of his belt, persuaded me to comply. The next day I turned up at school wearing my glasses.

'Specky four eyes! Specky four eyes!' taunted one of the biggest bullies at my school. I looked around when I heard his voice to see who his helpless victim might be. I hadn't realised he was calling me because I wasn't used to wearing glasses.

'What are you deaf as well, McFetridge?' he demanded, pushing his face into mine. 'Where'd you get them goggles, then?'

Blinking rapidly, I tried to think of something clever to say to make him laugh and so avoid a fight. But before I could even open my mouth, he had shoved me to the ground sending me sprawling onto the tarmac with a hard thud.

'Come on, four eyes,' he taunted. 'Stand up and fight.' As I struggled to my feet, a powerful fist slammed into my face sending my glasses flying. Blindly, I lunged forward and the two of us squirmed about in a heap with him on top until some kids warned us that a teacher was coming.

Blaming my teacher for this new affliction, I set about being even more unco-operative and withdrawn than I'd been previously. As a result, I left school branded as a failure for never having passed an exam but, more significantly, I left school with a hatred of all authority.

Now here I was faced with the one thing I'd thought I'd left behind me, and I could see the drill instructor was not going to relent until I'd obeyed him.

Suddenly I felt sick. By recklessly joining up I had let myself in for a worse persecution than I'd known at school. The situation was hopeless. As the PTI eyed me with contempt, waiting for me to obey his command to climb up a long, thick rope, something came over me. *I won't be beaten by this*, I thought.

'Give me that ****ing rope,' I spat back. With a gulp of air, I jumped up and began to tug my body up the rope a centimetre at a time. My feet felt like two anvils and my arms felt as if they would snap at any moment. A second later, I dropped onto the ground, sweating and huffing for breath. I jumped up again and wrestled with the rope, cursing as I strained to overcome gravity. Once more I dropped to the ground like a dead bird.

'Come on, sonny. Let's 'ave a go at press-ups,' the PTI said in a sadistic voice tinged with boredom.

I was beaten by the rope, but determined not to give in—even if I died in the process.

My initial attempts at the exercises were a joke, of course. I couldn't run, climb or do more than a few press-ups. But since it was clear to my PTI that I wanted to overcome my weak physical state, I was sent to a special training centre where I would train every day of the week.

At first, I couldn't keep up with the pace. But each day I threw myself into whatever task the PTIs set before me, and after several weeks of intensive physical training, I felt confident about my body for the first time ever. So much so, that by the time I was sent out to Ben Ghazi in Libya, North Africa, for my first tour of duty, I was ready for anything—anything, that is, except the boring life of a soldier which lay ahead of me.

# Chapter Four

From the very start to the last, army life was my worst enemy. It certainly was nothing like I'd imagined it to be. I suppose I expected a certain degree of mental stimulation as well as all the physical activities which made up my day-to-day existence. There was none. The only thing which kept me from losing my mind from boredom was drink. And it was drink which nearly killed me on the second day at my new camp.

Straightaway, I'd made friends with an Arab barman at a special pub for soldiers. It was my home away from home. On day two, I was the first customer in the bar. As the day wore on and the temperature rose steadily, I decided to take a bus down to the seaside for a swim.

I put on my swimming trunks, but I never got the chance to jump into the sea. I was so drunk by the time I had stumbled onto the beach, I decided to have a lie down and get a bit of sun instead. Within five minutes, I had passed out, staying unconscious for hours and missing the last bus back to the camp.

Eventually someone back at the camp noticed I was missing, so he returned to the beach looking for me. Meanwhile, beneath the equatorial sun, my body had ballooned and turned a dangerous shade of vermilion. After hours of literally frying in the sun, I was near death from acute sunstroke. The horrified soldier who found me had the good sense to rush me directly into hospital where I languished for a week, my face and body a mass of runny, red blisters and peeling, sun-damaged skin. To this day, I still have to take care to cover up on sunny days.

When I was fully recovered, I was called in by the head doctor who gave me a severe dressing down and threatened to put me on a charge since the incident was considered a self-inflicted wound. He must have taken pity on me, for in the end the matter was dropped and I returned to my squad without having charges pressed against me.

Although I was glad that the army had saved my life, I never felt I owed the army, or anyone associated with it, a debt of gratitude. It would be many years hence before I would learn about gratitude, so I continued to do as little work as possible, and to seek diversions with physical exercise, loose women, cheap booze and wild friends.

This was the Woodstock era: patriotism was a filthy word and while I wasn't a hippy, I partied with Arabs, Europeans and Americans every possible chance I had.

When I was transferred to Germany, I wondered if things might be different. But no, it was the same old story. My brain was atrophying at a rapid pace. I hated the regimented life of the army and literally marked time all week until I could get totally drunk at weekends. One of the perks of German life was that the beer was inexpensive and potent, and the bars seemed never to close.

In order to take advantage of the long opening hours of the pubs, a few of my friends and I found that it was a simple matter to sneak off base once we had checked in to our barracks for the night. Because of this, I could get up to no good several times a week.

I recall spending one night in a beer garden with several of my mates. A young American walked in and ordered a drink. 'Hey, you guys speak English? You mind if I drink with y'all?'

This guy was green, and we decided to have a bit of fun at his expense.

'Not at all,' I said, smiling. 'I hear Americans can out-drink anybody. Is that true?'

'Y'all better believe it, Buddy,' he replied, downing the contents of his beer stein. 'The next round's on me,' he said, pulling out a fat wad of marks. 'Matter of fact,' he bragged, 'I'm from St Louis, Missouri and we can out-drink anyone!'

'Is that a fact?' I replied with a wink at my friends and a sly nod at the money. After three more rounds for us, someone suggested a better bar across the street. 'Come on, Missouri,' we said. 'Let's go drink the Huns under the table.'

'You, sir, have got yourself a deal. Damn, you guys are really cool. This is my lucky night!'

What our American friend hadn't realised was that at the next bar, he was the only one drinking. We were merely holding half-full glasses. 'Another drink for Anglo-American unity,' someone had called out. 'Make it a beer with a shot of whisky.' After downing the beer followed by the neat whisky, the drunk and unstable soldier began to worry about how he'd find his way back to his base.

'Oh, don't worry about that,' I said. 'We'll take you back. You just enjoy yourself.' Not surprisingly, a few moments later, our friend from Missouri had passed out. Instantly, we helped ourselves to his money and then carried him out to the street where the damp night air revived him momentarily. 'I'll never forget you guys, believe me,' he muttered.

'And we'll never forget you,' I said. Then he passed out again. We left him snoring on a park bench.

I never gave the young soldier a second thought. In a way, we'd done him a favour by initiating him to life in Germany, for many a time my mates and I were on the receiving end of some very rough treatment as well.

One night we were drinking in a bar near Hamburg. The proprietor had a young daughter who had caught our eye. She was a pretty young thing, and all us lads took a fancy to her. After we had been drinking for several hours, the owner clearly wanted to close. So the Fraulein said in her thick German accent, 'You boys vill never get back alife in your condition. I call a taxi for you, *ja*?'

'*Ja, ja,*' we chimed back as we laughed and gulped down a few more neat whiskies as we waited.

Soon a man called from the door, 'You. Your taxi is ready! *Mach schnell*!' We stumbled out to the street and somebody shoved me into a car. That I got into the car, I'm certain. But that's all I can recall, for the next thing I knew it was nearly dawn, and I awoke stiff, sore, wet—and alone. I was at the bottom of a ditch underneath a hedge where I'd lain all night. Instinctively, I reached for my back pocket and, of course, my wallet was gone.

Often the misadventures I got up to were not only dangerous for me, but for anyone hapless enough to be with me.

For instance, one night when we were in England, a couple of my mates and I decided to see how fast we could drive a Land Rover through the centre of a Lancashire town.

Paying absolutely no attention to darting pedestrians or oncoming vehicles, the driver, a fellow Irishman, pressed his foot on the accelerator until we were roaring past a hedge near the edge of town at over fifty miles per hour. I was in the back of the Land Rover with three others, and we lads thought this was just great until the rear tyres skidded causing the vehicle to whip like a fish's tail. We reached frantically for something to hold on to, but to no avail: the sides and floor were sheer steel. Then gravity suddenly took on a will of its own, sending us crashing heavily into the ceiling, then back down to the floor and then, by way of the side wall, back to the ceiling again. At last we were dropped back to the floor where we all lay dazed and bloodied in a twisted heap. The vehicle had skidded and rolled over twice, stopping upright on the opposite side of the hedge. The Land Rover was written off and one of my mates lost an eye as a result of that crash.

Two police cars arrived on the scene and we were arrested. And despite our colluded story that a dog had run out in front of our vehicle as we rushed back to camp so as not to be late, we were punished by the army with fines and prison.

This, then, was my life: one long cycle of skiving at work, partying at the weekend, and paying stiff fines or doing time in military prisons, or, more often than not, both, as punishment for behaviour unbecoming to a member of Her Majesty's armed forces.

Gradually, I found that booze alone was not

enough to give me the thrill I was seeking, so I started smoking pot. At first, one or two cigarettes rolled out of this fragrant weed would give me the buzz of eight pints of beer or half-a-pint of whisky. Soon, however, I needed more and more marijuana to attain the all-important high. Mercifully, despite my using all sorts of drugs, I never got hooked on the really hard stuff, although many of my close mates were heroin addicts by the age of twenty.

Around this time, I became addicted to another sort of substance: pornography. As a youngster in Larne, I had seen girly magazines, of course, but after one look at the hard-core stuff, I was hooked. After a while, I was spending plenty of money buying up pornographic magazines and films. I enjoyed looking at this material myself, but another reason why I bought it was that it was virtually unobtainable in Northern Ireland in those days, and I was able to resell it for five times what I paid when I went back to Larne. The problem of pornography would raise its head once again in my life once I was behind bars in Ulster some years hence. Then I was a Christian and had inner resources to break this addiction. Meanwhile, I continued to live in a world of sexual fantasy, buying and selling some really sordid material. One more thing about my addiction to pornography: I realise now that my ideas about sex were all polluted by violent and demeaning material and for anyone to argue that pornography has no effect on male attitudes towards women is fallacious.

The awful truth about porn is that the more you see of it, the more you need it to fulfil your pleasures. I completely disagree that pornography serves some purpose to society by allowing men to relieve themselves of sexual tensions. All it does is frustrate, and in the end it inspires people to act out the lewdest fantasies on other human beings. After a while, normal sexual relations are impossible to maintain. This I learned the hard way.

In those days, I must have fancied myself as something of a gangster because I bought myself a couple of gas pistols and pellets. I liked them because they looked like real pistols and I could show off with them without breaking any laws. A friend of mine called Murphy, a Roman Catholic from Dublin, bought a gas pistol from me and got caught with it. Somehow the police had linked Murphy's gas pistol with some other real guns which had been smuggled from Germany. In the end, unbeknown to me, he grassed on me and was cleared. Soon after, however, the police had picked me up for questioning. I wasn't worried, though, for a gas pistol is a relatively harmless pellet gun and hardly a dangerous weapon. My nonchalance turned to genuine fear when I learned that the police suspected I was running guns from the Continent for the UDA. Furthermore, they suspected that my sole reason for making friends with Murphy was to lure him to Larne in order to murder him as a hated Roman Catholic. I had the good fortune of being let off as the police's suspicions couldn't be proved. Even this close brush with the international law did little to dampen my wild ways.

I can't recall how many days and weeks I spent in jail as a result of my rowdy life, but when it was time for me to be discharged from the army, by the grace of God, my commanding officer offered to give me a satisfactory dismissal. 'McFetridge,' he said, 'if you can stay out of trouble for the last few weeks of your time with me, I promise I won't give you a dis-honourable discharge, although looking over your record, you richly deserve to be kicked out and branded as the troublemaker you really are.'

I shrugged and mumbled, 'Yes, sir.' I couldn't believe my good luck. A dishonourable discharge would have haunted me for the rest of my life, making it impossible to find a decent job, or to point to my time in the Forces as proof of my maturity and ability to work hard. Again, I felt no gratitude for a kindness done freely to me. All I could think of was the impending freedom which lay ahead of me once I was out of the army.

True to the commander's promise, my discharge papers gave me a satisfactory rating, but they listed in red the number of fines I had paid for my wild ways. Tallying up the fines—ten pounds here, twenty pounds there—I reckon that I must have paid out thousands of pounds during my six years in the army. For the first time ever, I felt ashamed of myself. The army life was no life for me.

For all these reasons, then, when the Larne UDA representatives headhunted me because they thought I'd make a tough and disciplined leader of a paramilitary organisation by virtue of my having been a soldier, I felt like bursting out laughing. I hated the army, and I had no desire to put myself back under someone else's authority so soon after demobbing. And yet something deep inside me was saying, 'Join up!' For one thing, the deaths of Jim and Tom, as well as a dozen others whom I'd known, always lurked at the back of my mind. Didn't their blood cry out for revenge? One thing I did know for certain: I couldn't sit on the fence much longer.

# Chapter Five

By the end of 1973, families were being shattered daily by the unrest in Belfast. Many parts of the city, such as the Falls Road and Andersontown, had become virtual no-go areas. Belfast wasn't the only place where unrest was rife. Violence knew no geographic boundary. Even in tiny Larne, one section of the town was renamed 'Boyne Square' and Catholics were wise to steer clear of there if they knew what was good for them. And although it was only a tiny minority of Roman Catholics and Protestants who were doing most of the killings, these same people seemed to be the only ones doing anything about the stalemate between the factions in Ireland.

The IRA had declared war on Great Britain, and their battlefield was Ulster. Their sole goal was to get Britain out of Ireland and to reabsorb Ulster into the Southern Republic. The aims of the Ulster paramilitary organisations were also clearly defined and simple: to protect the interests and traditions of the six counties of Northern Ireland; to bring justice to the North; and to ensure that Ulster remained Protestant and British.

For Irish terrorists on both sides of the divide, daily injustices set an agenda of civil war and justified in the minds of many the use of violence to bring about change.

I knew that it would be a matter of time before I had to make my intentions known to the local UDA members: either I would decline their offer to join up and then leave Northern Ireland to work abroad, for there would be no peace for me if I remained in Ulster, or I would join the ranks and pick up the gun for the Protestant cause. The one commodity I was rapidly running out of was time.

It might be worthwhile at this point to explain a few details about Ulster and my home town of Larne. First of all, unless you live here, it's impossible to comprehend the full measure of bitter feeling which permeates this troubled land. To better comprehend the problem as it exists today, you need to go back many years before the British Forces were committed to Northern Ireland in 1969. It's necessary to consider briefly certain events which took place in Ulster between 1912 and 1914.

In those days, the whole of Ireland was ruled from London. The Irish party at Westminster had advocated 'Home Rule' for Ireland with a parliament in Dublin. That object seemed about to come to pass in 1912 after the Liberals passed the Home Rule Bill in the Commons. Though it was rejected by the House of Lords, all the pundits were predicting that the law would be enacted by 1914.

The Bill proposed that limited control be given to the new parliament in Dublin. This Bill, while a satisfactory compromise in the eyes of the English, was riddled with problems for the Irish. The Southern Irish wanted full control of a united Ireland. To those in the North, the idea of Home Rule was seen as a threat by Ulster Unionists who feared that a parliament controlled by a majority of Catholics would threaten their religious heritage as well as upset the free trade between Ulster and Britain. This latest proposal was merely added fuel to the fire under the kettle which was Ireland.

Northern resistance to Home Rule was organised by a Dublin barrister called Sir Edward Carson, who organised large public meetings to oppose it. In September of 1912, 400,000 people signed a covenant in Belfast's City Hall, agreeing to fight Home Rule at all costs. The Ulster Unionists drew up a plan for a Provisional Government in the North in case of an emergency. By January 1913, the Ulster Volunteer Force (UVF) was created should an armed struggle be necessary to ensure continued union with Westminster.

The objectives of the UVF were similar to today's UDA (Ulster Defence Association): armed resistance to Home Rule by Dublin. A familiar slogan daubed on walls in Larne at that time was: 'Home Rule is Rome Rule'.

In the spring of 1914, Home Rule was thought by many to be a *fait accompli*, hence the UVF undertook desperate steps to defend their territory. During the night of 24th April 1914, 40,000 rifles and 5 million rounds of ammunition were carried ashore in Larne from the hold of the ship 'Mountjoy'. A poem written at the time records the event:

43

> Who ran the guns, when landed
> From Larne, North, South and West,
> Through a vigil-keeping Ulster,
> That had known that night no rest?
> 'Twas the gallant men of Ulster—
> Then away with talk and cant,
> For all are of the self-same breed
> Who signed the Covenant.

Local Ulster Volunteers sealed off all approaches to Larne Harbour making it impossible for the police to interfere had they so desired. The law enforcers merely looked the other way as a vast fleet of motor cars, lorries and wagons turtled up to the quayside and received their booty and then disappeared into the misty night to distribute the arms into eager hands in every part of Ulster. By 2am, the job was accomplished. Unmolested, the 'Mountjoy' eased out into the harbour and unloaded the remainder of its cargo in Bangor.

This landing of arms gave rise to a series of private armies all over Northern Ireland. Not waiting for shots to be fired, Roman Catholics formed the Irish National Volunteers (INV) whose *raison d'etre* was to oppose their Protestant counterparts. It was roughly the equivalent of today's Provisional IRA. An armed confrontation was imminent. All that was needed now was the signing into law of the Home Rule Act.

In fact, the Home Rule Act was not passed at that time because of another civil war which had erupted thousands of miles away in Sarajevo, Yugoslavia, following the assassination of Archduke Franz Ferdinand. Of course this was the main event which led to the outbreak of the First World War in August 1914. An emergency bill was passed in Parliament to suspend the Home Rule Act. Armed and trained for battle, many of the Ulster Volunteer Force and the Irish National Volunteers went to Europe to fight with Britain against Germany; hence a bloody civil war in Ireland was averted—for the time being.

In 1916, while the war was waging in far off Europe, a group of Irish Catholics led by James Connolly staged an armed rebellion in the South. The uprising began in O'Connell Street, Dublin. After a few weeks, the rebellion was put down and its leaders were killed or arrested. Nevertheless, the events of April 1916 had fanned the flames of Irish nationalism and Dublin became the epicentre of Irish political unity, with the leaders of the Dublin uprising cast as modern martyrs for the cause of Irish autonomy.

In 1918, a general election was held and the majority elected party, Sinn Fein, came into power and set up a parliament in Dublin against the wishes of Britain. After two years of bitterness and fighting, the British Government gave in to the pressure in July 1921 and passed an Act dividing Ireland into two parts. Six counties in Northern Ireland were to remain as part of Great Britain, and the remaining twenty-six in the south became The Irish Free State (Southern Ireland).

Understandably, neither side was fully satisfied with this compromise, and the rest is the history of two people bound together but determined not to accept the status quo.

George Santayana once said that those who cannot remember the past are condemned to repeat it, but in Ulster it is those who *do* remember the past who are repeating history—and they are forcing others to relive it as well.

Each day that passed, I asked myself: 'Should I join up or should I sit on the fence?' The answer to that question, hinged on one thing: 'Did I hate Roman Catholics enough to take up arms against them?' Casting my mind back over the years, I realised that a good many of my friends were Catholic. Then an ugly incident came to mind like an unwanted guest.

It happened in 1969 when I was twenty. I had joined with my mates and had become an Apprentice Boy—a thing all young men in Ulster are encouraged to do. Although I wasn't particularly religious or patriotic, I felt proud to take the solemn oaths of allegiance to God, the Order and my country. It was during the mass parade in Derry, while the bands marched and we were about to be made Apprentice Boys inside the Guild Hall there, that they reckon the so-called recent troubles began. I'd noticed an unusually heavy police presence throughout the day, but I took no special notice until after the ceremony when we were parading through the Diamond in Derry. Suddenly, a mob of teenaged boys pressed in close, cursing and laughing at us. A police cordon was formed to keep us apart. Within seconds all us lads were being pelted by stones and missiles launched by a gang the police said had come from Roman Catholic Bogside.

I remember a lad in our parade broke rank, and charged through the crowd trying to get his hands on one of the troublemakers. But before he could turn down the passage where they had retreated, a big police sergeant reached out a massive hand and grabbed him by the collar and shouted, 'Hey, where're you going?' The newly-made Apprentice Boy replied that he was going after the retreating Catholics. 'Aye, that's just what they want you to do.

Don't you know that if you go down there you'll not be coming back?' I was shocked by his words. Did he really mean that the boys meant to kill him? Instantaneously, shock gave way to anger that the police didn't chase them. They had insulted our banner. They had injured us with rocks. Indeed, they meant to murder any one of us. I wondered why the police were letting them get away with this.

You might say that after this incident I detested Roman Catholics, and in a way I did; but my hatred of Catholics was very selective, for soon after that I began to date Catholic girls in Larne.

When my dad heard about my girlfriends, his gruff comment was, 'So our Protestant girls aren't good enough, then?' Oddly enough, the parents of the Catholic girls I knew completely accepted me for who and what I was. For Catholic boys, though, I think there was strong resentment when Protestants lured their girls away, just as I know there was among Protestant boys when the shoe was on the other foot.

It's said that in Ireland, the people live with history in their pockets; it's something we carry around with us. Ireland has known hundreds of years of national and sectarian strife. In the past, the surest way to bring about peace was by force, even if the peace was nothing more than the mere absence of outward conflict. To be perfectly honest, I couldn't see any way other than armed conflict to bring about an end to the sea of problems facing Irish Protestants. For one thing, nobody knew of a workable political solution: the IRA wanted reunification with the South, and the UDA wanted to remain loyal to the Crown. So it was a stalemate. Oh, there were a few simpering Christians running about in those days talking of reconciliation and the need to forgive, but as far as I could see, they were religious fanatics whose God was their opium, to paraphrase Marx. And anyway, the churches weren't all preaching this soppy 'forgive and forget' philosophy. The Revd Ian Paisley was invoking the Christian God to smite the heretical Papists 'hip and thigh', and more than one Catholic priest was aiding and abetting known IRA killers. In those uncertain days, of one thing I was convinced: that of all people in the world, Christians were the least likely to solve Ulster's problems.

Still, I knew that nothing was less excusable than a war due to prejudice—I had learned this as a soldier. But I hadn't gone seeking this conflict; it had sought me. First a member of my family had been killed by the IRA, then the UDA had invited me to join with them.

It was useless to try to sit on the fence and pretend everything was just fine. At last, I decided that I would join the UDA. The following week, I was a fully-fledged member of the Ulster Defence Association. I was so naive, I believed that the UDA could do in six months what the British presence had been unable to do in six years. So did most of my fellow soldiers. Nothing could have been further from the truth. Today, some twenty-two years later, the armed struggle continues and neither side seems any closer to a workable solution to the problem.

Frequently, my involvement in the UDA seemed to me to be a ridiculous sham: instead of being the brave freedom fighters we claimed to be, we were more like Chicago-style mobsters. In the end, we began to justify using violence against Protestants if need be, in order to keep our cause alive; moreover, the IRA were doing much the same thing. More than once innocent Roman Catholics were killed by Republican bombs or bullets.

It was thoughts like these which dogged me from time to time, making me think perhaps the whole cause was worthless. Be that as it may, at the end of the day, at least I was trying to do something about the problem of injustice, even if by doing so I was contributing to other injustices.

During those early hours after the incident at Larne Football Club, I knew it would be only a matter of time before I stopped a bullet with my name on it or was nicked and possibly ended up in prison for good.

That night, I lay smoking in the dark until I could hear the bells of Larne tolling 2am. Undressing, I curled down into the blankets and sighed. At this stage there was no backing out. I knew too much and had become too deeply involved to drop out. It was a *fait accompli*. Besides, I had plenty of work to do when the sun came up. Turning onto my side, I closed my eyes and immediately the curtain of sleep drew across my mind.

# Chapter Six

Because I was seen as fearless and macho, I quickly rose in the paramilitary ranks, which meant I was busy nearly every evening of the week with robberies, shootings or making plans for more mayhem. In the mid to late 1970s, there was an active attempt on the part of the paramilitaries to infiltrate the UDR (Ulster Defence Regiment) which is the local army regiment here in Northern Ireland. I was urged to make a formal application. This I did. Had I or any other of my mates in the UDA got into the ranks of the UDR, we could have had access to the security forces' classified information which would have been a great boon to the UDA's own campaign. My 'illustrious' army record must have been scrutinised, because my application was tersely rejected.

Even though I was in the UDA, I still needed a job. As I've already said, I seemed to drift from one thing to another—washing dishes, working in the docks, factory work. At one point I was a guard for Securicor.

While I was a guard, I carried around more

money in one sack than my mates and I could pinch in a month. But never once did I succumb to the temptation to steal from Securicor. Not that I was an honest employee, mind you; it's just that I knew I would be caught and sent to prison. Besides, I was more interested in our cause than in thieving.

One evening, I picked up the telephone and rang a contact. 'Billy here. Meet me at the usual place at 9pm, and bring along the stuff.' The 'stuff', as my contact well knew, was an alarm clock and explosive materials—a homemade bomb we were going to test that night. If we happened to score a success with our latest formula, we would proceed to build enough homemade bombs to terrorise every Roman Catholic within a thirty-mile radius of Larne.

More and more, my parents' flat was, for all intents and purposes, becoming an integral UDA headquarters where guns and bombs were routinely kept. Hence, I needed to take great care. I never knew when someone might be eavesdropping either on my end or the other. My parents may have suspected that I was up to no good, but if they did they never let on. To be sure, I kept my comings and goings strictly private and was at pains never to abuse their hospitality.

In a funny sort of way, being at home after six years in the army was almost like a second chance to relive my childhood, only now I was an adult.

On the whole, mine was a far from perfect childhood, even though compared to many others it was happy enough. In the early 1950s, there were no council flats in Larne. We lived in a plain, whitewashed house in Meeting House Street. There were scores of kids in this neighbourhood where parents worked hard, and looked after each other's needs. The focal point of the Ulster year then as today was the July holidays and the week leading up to 12th July. There was dancing in the streets with everyone wearing orange, and it was then I had my first taste of alcohol—all in good fun, mind you. This was years before the troubles were to flare up in Derry in 1969, but I suppose to onlooking Roman Catholics our high-jinks might have seemed a wee bit intimidating. After all, the whole point of the celebrations was to mark the decline of the Roman Catholic influence and the rise of Protestantism back around 1795. Over the years, it became synonymous with union with Britain and a Protestant show of solidarity. In a way, one might compare the feelings of the Catholic community then to those of pre-Civil Rights black America. Then, blacks played almost no role in politics, education and law, and when they did, they were usually seen as suspect. Likewise, in British Ulster, Roman Catholics knew they were barred from marrying into the Royal Family, and there was a tacit agreement among many Protestant law-makers, employers and educators to discriminate against them. But as I say, no thought whatsoever was given during the July festivities as to how our Catholic neighbours might have felt when the music got louder and the drinks were freely flowing.

While most families in our street had four or five children as the norm, the McFetridge household had only me and my sister. My mother became pregnant again when I was about four or five. How I hoped for a younger brother with whom I could play! I longed for Mum to get on with it. Then at last came the fateful day when my dad took me to her bedside, saying there was someone they wanted me to meet. I won't say I was disappointed when Mum told me the baby's name was Betty, but I wasn't ecstatic, either. For better or worse, I had a baby sister. In time, Betty and I were to become as close as any two brothers ever were—partly out of familial love, but partly, too, out of a mutual understanding that we needed each other to survive the harsh conditions in the streets and at home—especially as we related to my dad.

Some of the highlights of my childhood centred around the times Betty and I played football or hide-and-seek in the streets of Larne. As I said, she was to become the brother I never had and, since I was her elder, I became her protector when she ran afoul of the street bullies, of which there were plenty. I wasn't a very sturdy boy, and because my eyes were very weak, more often than not I took a few hard knocks on Betty's behalf, but it was worth it. In return for my bruises and lumps, I gained Betty's affection which I craved as a plant craves water in a dry spell.

As close as we two were, I'm afraid as we grew up, Betty became a rival for my father's attention which I resented bitterly. At home my father was continually praising and rewarding Betty. I felt not only had I been denied a male companion my own age, but owing to Betty's charm, I was also denied the male companionship of my father. Betty had clearly won the war for Dad's affection; and I had lost. I compensated for this by becoming something of a mama's boy. I did this more out of my craving for affirmation than my having a naturally loving nature.

Consequently, a love-hate situation developed among my sister, my parents and myself which never truly disappeared until we were all grown up and out of the family home.

One thing I found terribly upsetting stemmed from the fact that whenever we children were bad, we were given hard blows by my father with the strap, and while he didn't beat us unmercifully, he was only too ready to remove his wide, black belt and use it on our little legs when we played up. The result was I developed a deep fear of my father; a fear that he would beat me, or that he might one day really hurt my sister whom I felt duty-bound to defend, as I've said.

I deeply resented my father's hypocrisy. Once when I was twelve he caught me smoking. Off came the belt and he began to lay down the law. This time I decided to dig my heels in. 'Look, Dad,' I shouted. 'You smoke, Mum smokes, so I'll smoke too.' The rebellion was short-lived; I got the belt, hard and fast, and any smoking I did after that had to be done sneakily.

In the main, my father limited his cross words and beatings to us children. To his mates and to other families in our street he was as good natured as could be. What's more, he was civil, almost loving, to our mother.

Only once in those years did I see him angry enough to threaten my mother physically. One evening he demanded his tea after having been in the pub for most of the day. I was about fourteen years old at the time and was in the living room from where I could hear his shouts getting louder and louder. To me, it sounded alarmingly as if he was about to beat my mother. At last, I couldn't take it any longer, and I ran to the back kitchen where they were. Stepping into the fray, I pulled myself up to my full height and, thrusting out my chest, I roared into my father's face, 'If you so much as lay a hand on Mum, I swear I'll kill you!' I braced myself for his blow, or at least his angry retort. But to my utter astonishment, my father's reaction was not the belt, nor was it a string of obscenities. Instead, he looked at me and began to cry. Later he said he had never laid a hand on our mother and that he never would. That was all that happened. Not another word was said of the incident.

A few days later I was thinking about my threat. I was upset and confused about my readiness to kill, or threaten to kill, my father.

My father drank fairly heavily and was stern and not very talkative in the home. When he did feel abusive, he criticised me. Even if someone said something good about me (a rarity), he was quick to pour cold water on that sort of thing. He'd say, 'Billy's no good, and he'll never amount to anything.' This cut me to the bone. I wondered if it was true that I was 'no good'. From my adolescent point of view, there seemed plenty of evidence to support this notion: I was no good at school, no good at sport. I began to believe that my father was right. The strange thing is his words didn't really hurt me. They were apparently fact. But what did hurt was that he never once said the words, 'Son, I love you.' For in my mind, even if I was no good, I belonged to my father. I was his son. Did my father love me?

I gather he did love me, in his own way, because of a few isolated incidents when I was a boy.

Once he took me along while he drank in the pub. After he'd had a few rounds, he began to brag about me. Not that there was much to brag about, for as a baby I was sickly and nearly died—the result of being a 'blue baby' during a home birth. And although I was tall for my age, and I enjoyed playing football and rounders, I was an awkward child with very weak eyes. Because of this I wasn't very good at sport. But all the same, my father got it into his head to brag about me. 'Aye, do you see our Billy?' he suddenly proclaimed to a line of working men at the bar. 'He's got great potential, great potential!' I pulled myself up and positively glowed at this, even if his mates' eyes told me they didn't seem overly impressed by a scrawny boy who squinted as he stood there nursing a ginger beer. I waited for him to say what my great potential was, but the old man just dropped the subject, and I slouched back against the cold rim of the bar.

Another time I felt he loved me because he took me to fish with him. My father loved to fish. And while he had no patience in the home, when he was sitting on the bank of a river with his fishing pole in hand, he'd patiently sit and wait for a nibble until dark. On the face of it, this was a chance for us to do some male bonding. The trouble was I hated fishing.

In order to please him I agreed to go, but I found sitting next to the old man in complete silence hour after hour absolutely unbearable. I would snatch sidelong glances at him, trying to fathom what could be going on in his mind as he sat statue-like on the river bank. He never moved nor spoke. My back itched, my shoulders ached and I was cold. I'd much rather have been running around in the fields or skipping rocks on the surface of the river, but I dared not, for that would spoil Dad's fishing. A week later, I refused his second offer to go fishing which must have annoyed him because we never fished together again.

My fondest memory of my father occurred sometime after I had been arrested and put in prison. The first time he came up to see me, we sat and made polite small talk. I don't recall how long he stayed nor what passed between us two, but as he got up to leave, he reached out and hugged me. I was thirty years old, and that was the first and only time in my life that he had shown any tender feelings towards me. In my mind, I wondered if this would be the beginning of a new relationship with him. Unfortunately, my father died one month before I left prison and our chance to establish a loving rapport had passed for good.

On the other hand, Mum always loved us children, and gave us everything Betty or I asked for if it were within her power. Most of the time, all she had to offer us was her love, but this was what Betty and I wanted most of all, so not having all the fine toys or the new bikes that some of our neighbours had wasn't too awful for we felt loved and that did wonders for us.

I know that despite my father's gruff exterior, Mum loved him. They went out every Saturday night, and I recall they often came home with friends and there would be a party in our living room. They drank and played records, party music we used to call it; Orange music and the like. Mum liked for us children to join in and have whatever good food or drinks were available, so many's the night when Betty and I were fetched from our beds to join in with the adults until we were too tired to stay awake. It was important to my mother that we children knew how special we were to her.

She was this way even in the days when I was running guns in Larne. That's why it was sort of special to be back under her roof once again.

I can't say I was able to return her affection quite as readily. I was a taker, more's the pity. I even had the audacity to ask my mother to knit me the black balaclava which I used for my work with the UDA. I honestly don't think she ever suspected what serious crimes I got up to in that warm and lovingly-knit item—even after my arrest. Mothers are like that, I guess. Bless 'em!

The morning after the shooting, I was preparing to test a bomb I wanted to use in Larne. At the agreed time and place, I met with my mate whom I'll call Geoff.

'Look what I got here,' he said, revealing a gap-toothed smile which ran from ear lobe to ear lobe.

Eagerly, I reached into the sack he was carrying and held a squat pipe bomb in my hands. On one end was a simple alarm clock, and on the other was a series of wires. Inside the pipe was about half-a-pound of assorted chemicals and gunpowder. This was in the days before semtex and today's other sophisticated plastic explosives.

'Will she blow?' I asked.

'Dunno,' came the awkward reply. 'Want to try it here?'

I nodded. Taking the pipe bomb out to the centre of a large bit of wasteland outside Larne, I set it on a tree stump and crouched down. I looked at my wristwatch: it was 10.40. I set the alarm for 10.45 and calmly strolled back to where Geoff stood waiting. 'We had better move off to the wood in case

59

the bang brings the police snooping around,' I commented.

Nervously, I eyed my watch. The second hand was sweeping towards the twelve. In a few seconds we would know if our formula would work. If the experiment was successful, we could then wage a time-bomb campaign against Catholic shops and known IRA safehouses in our area. I looked at my cocked wrist again and was dismayed to see that the second hand had now swept past the twelve and was making its descent to the four.

'Wait,' I said, 'give her a few seconds more. She's bound to blow.'

I could see Geoff frown. A full minute passed, and then another minute and thirty seconds more passed before I spoke again. 'It's a dud. Back to the drawing board, I guess, eh, Geoff? Just run along and pick it up, will you?' I said.

'M-me?'

'Yeah, it's a dud. It won't go off now. It was set to blow a full three minutes ago.' I made a slow move towards the bomb to show him I wasn't afraid. Reluctantly, he moved on ahead of me.

Prudently, I stopped and scanned the nearby road in case any unwanted visitors might arrive on the scene while we were there. Then I glanced back at Geoff who was about ten feet away from the bomb. He seemed to be turning his head and was about to call out something to me when an almighty *ba-boom* split the tranquillity of the night. A dull thud echoed off the hills in the distance. Geoff was knocked over by the force, but was soon on his feet scampering back towards me. We both knew that the noise would bring a swarm of police to the area in just a few minutes.

'Are you all right?' I asked as we made a dash back to the woods.

'Yeah,' he puffed. 'That was loud! I think we have a winner there. All we need is a clock that keeps better time!'

'Let's get out of here,' I said, turning on my heels.

As we trotted along, we became aware of a low rumbling somewhere in the night sky. Suddenly the rumbling was overhead and almost deafening. There were searchlights from above. An army helicopter had been dispatched. We didn't have to think twice about what was to be done—we disappeared into the woods. Oddly enough, had the police arrived in cars they might very well have caught us that time. As they were in the sky, it was a simple matter to stick to the fields and woods and then resurface back in Larne with nobody the wiser.

This, then, was my life. In a bizzare sense it gave me meaning, fulfilment and a sense of destiny, even if I knew my destiny might be a cold prison cell or a six-foot hole in the ground one day sooner rather than later.

Somehow, in the midst of all my activities, I found a night job. Or more accurately, a night job found me. In fact, this job would eventually lead to another one which is where I met Christine, the woman who was to become my first wife.

## Chapter Seven

My new job started when one of Securicor's clients
spotted me while I was on duty at his place of
business, a hotel near Belfast. He was a successful
businessman. I could feel his intense gaze which he
had locked onto me, but I kept my stony face firmly
fixed on the sack of money I was guarding. For all I
knew, he might have been a supergrass who recognised me as a UDA ringleader.

As I was leaving the premises, he stopped me.
'You ever do any night work?' he asked.

'You mean with the company?'

'No, I mean on your own time.'

I was cool and stared blankly into his olive
coloured eyes. 'Let me explain,' he added with a
laugh. 'I could use a bloke like you to keep an eye on
my customers. You know, a bouncer, like.'

Relaxing, I said, 'I never tried anything like that.'

'I'll pay you cash. You look like you'll do just fine.
And if you're a clever lad, you'll find work in other
nightclubs.'

The promise of easy money was more than I

could resist, so I began a new career as a security man at local nightclubs.

I really enjoyed the job which was about 90% play acting—you know, Mr Macho, tough as ten miles of barbed wire—and 10% work. As a result of my oscar-winning posing, very few customers gave me any stick. Soon I was working for most of the hotels all over Ulster.

Night after night I could have as many drinks as I wanted. I got to meet women, and I even danced with a few, getting down to the driving rhythm of the local rock bands who did gigs at the night spots. Life couldn't have been better. That is, until I met another guy who had a sweeter business offer which I couldn't refuse.

His idea was to do the promoting of the music groups as well as to set up gigs and discos. While many of the bands in Ulster during the mid-1970s were quite talented, very few knew how to manage their careers properly. That's where we came in. The job involved a bit of salesmanship as well as doing bookings for the groups. The pay was to be a direct cut of the band's takings. Sometimes there was plenty, other times there wasn't. The best bit, though, was that someone else did the work while I got paid for it. The lure of easy money proved more than I could resist.

The next three years, from 1977 until my arrest in late 1980, were the most fulfilling since I'd left the army in 1973. For once in my life I had a job that allowed me to be my own boss. It was a job which required a clean suit and shirt and no bending, shoving or putting my health at risk for someone else's profit. I had a chance to create a new name and image for myself. What's more, it looked like it would be steady money as long as I took the business side of it seriously.

As I've said already, I was slowly becoming disillusioned with my UDA work, and with this new night job I was able to ease up legitimately on my commitment to terrorism. I wanted a break, and this was my big chance. To my relief, there was tacit agreement from my officers for me to go on leave for a time.

While working at a dance along the Antrim Coast early in 1977, I met my first wife, Christine. I had been introduced to her by a friend who was looking to make a threesome into a foursome. I was normally wary of blind dates, and I was certainly not hard up for female companionship, but I have to say that Christine and I really hit it off quite well— better, in fact, than the other couple we were with.

That night the four of us danced, drank and laughed, but for Christine and me, we might have been completely alone. We had eyes only for each other.

It was a matter of three or four months before I realised I'd like to marry Christine. I knew she felt the same about me. So one night in my flat, I decided to pop the question. To my intense relief she said yes. At the ripe old age of twenty-seven, I was to become a married man.

In the April of 1977 Christine and I were married in a Presbyterian church in Larne, and our first home was in the high rise flats at Riverdale. Looking back now, I suppose if I had really thought it through, neither of us were ready for marriage at the time, not least of all because of our financial situation. Despite my promotion work, I'd never learned to save money. I spent whatever I earned as fast as it came into my hands. Christine knew this, but couldn't stop my being a spendthrift. I think maybe she thought that one day she would change me. Anyway, we were young and our heads were stuffed with all sorts of romantic ideas about how a marriage is supposed to work.

Maybe it would be more accurate to say I was the one who was full of romantic ideas, for Christine was far more level-headed than I was. She worked hard to make a home, and if I'd have been another sort of man, it might have worked out just fine. But because I worked nights away from home, I began messing around in ways that a married man should never even contemplate.

Night after night I would be in one club or another, ostensibly looking after my business interests, but in point of fact I was hanging around the bar drinking and flirting with the waitresses.

Many nights I'd work until the small hours of the morning, but instead of packing up with the band and getting home to Christine, I'd agree to play a hand or two of cards with the hotel night workers. Other times I'd have drunk far too much to drive home, so I'd stay in a room to sleep it off.

Of course, having easy access to private bedrooms, it wasn't long before I'd be chatting up some of the waitresses with an eye to a few hours of quick sex. I suppose to most of the women I appeared to be a big-time promotion man. To me, they appeared to be young, nubile and eager. In any case, we all seemed to have the same thing on our minds.

The saddest thing is, despite my affairs, I was in love with Christine, and I had no cause to want sex outside of my marriage. She was a good wife and a good lover. I was acting out of compulsion to be seen as a big man; a man who knew what he wanted and knew how to get it. Aside from that, there had been a big sexual revolution in the 1960s and 70s. It was the done thing to cheat on your spouse. Many of the women with whom I slept had husbands of their own who were no doubt out having sex somewhere else. AIDS was unheard of in Britain in those days, and I shudder now when I think of how close we all were to this modern epidemic which now adds a deadly physical dimension to a deadly spiritual malady.

I was in a different town every week, and before long I had a network of sleeping partners. To some men, this might sound like an enviable lifestyle, for what man has never fantasised about having his very own harem of young women all at his beck and call? But it isn't like you may think. After a while you get fed up with it all; you get tired of your favourite women and begin looking for new ones to take their place. A man may as well drink salt water to quench his thirst, though, because the more you have the less it satisfies. Even when Christine announced that we were to have a baby, I carried on as badly as ever.

During those years I kept up with my UDA work, although it took up less time than before. It was a precarious balancing act, and in the back of my mind I knew the police would catch up with me, but the bitterness in my heart against Catholics goaded me on and on, causing me to be involved in some fairly risky acts. Acts that would affect not only me, but also Christine or our families.

Although to the outside world there appears to be unity and cohesion among the paramilitaries, there is in fact inside feuding and rivalry. Like Chicago mobsters, two or more terrorists may band together in order to kill another hated member. I know about this from first-hand experience.

Apparently, some months earlier, I'd been flirting with the wife of a fellow UDA terrorist whom I'll call Phil. He was none too pleased, because one night a bomb was planted outside the door of my mother's flat in Larne. Of course, this was a stupid move if Phil really intended to kill me, because my comings and goings there were erratic.

Not surprisingly, it was my poor mother who suffered the night the bomb had been planted. That evening she had been out for a drink with my father. For some reason, Dad was walking a few feet behind Mum, so she was the first to reach the door to the flat.

As it happens, there is a heavy wooden fire door at the beginning of the corridor to their flat. Giving the heavy door a hefty tug, my mother jammed her foot into the opening at the same instant the bomb exploded.

She was severely shaken by the bomb and certainly would have been killed had she not been standing behind the sturdy door which absorbed the full impact of the blast. Mercifully she was not harmed, and suffered only holes in her tights.

The police questioned us about the bomb; about who might have planted it and why, but they never suspected that I was a terrorist. The whole matter was treated like a civilian murder attempt on my life. That suited me, for I didn't want the police to snoop into my paramilitary affairs.

I had a fairly clear idea of who my would-be murderer was. After a few of my mates confronted Phil, the whole matter was cleared up, and I was back flirting with the ladies—but not his wife!

Some jobs I did for the UDA, I thought up myself; others were the result of orders which filtered down to me from some nameless, faceless voice on the other end of a phone.

In June of 1980, I was ordered to follow a man I'll call John Smith; a man whom I knew personally.

After a number of missions, I failed to find my man. I was so cold-hearted in those days that I never even thought about Smith's fate. Was he going to be killed? Would they just 'rough him up'? I didn't know; nor did I care. Was I guilty of self-deception? That was part of it, but looking back knowing what I now know, I believe that I was fully under the influence of dark powers greater than most people, even many theologians, understand. (I think the American novelist, Frank Peretti and editors C Peter Wagner and F Douglas Pennoyer hit the nail on the head as they explore spiritual warfare and its influence on human activities. I recommend that you try to read their books for insights into this little understood area.[1])

The Smith job involved following my victim and making notes of his movements. He frequented a hotel which was known to me, but he eluded me somehow.

On the night of Smith's murder, I drove to a hotel where I was working. On the Coast Road I was stopped at a road block.

'Identification, please,' ordered the police officer.

---

[1] Frank Peretti, *This Present Darkness* and *Piercing the Darkness* (Minstrel: Eastbourne), 1990; C Peter Wagner, F Douglas Pennoyer, eds, *Wrestling With Dark Angels* (Monarch: Eastbourne), 1990.

Without a word, I handed over my driving licence.

'Right,' was his only reply as he handed back my property and waved me on.

*That was easy*, I thought to myself. *Would that all cops were as easy-going as he is.* Ironically, it was that policeman's spot check which would be my undoing in under three months' time. What's more, even though I wasn't the gunman, Smith's death would eventually be pinned on me, along with other crimes which I hadn't committed. But I'll come to that later.

By the time I got home to the flats it was after 3am. I never even considered how Christine might have felt being alone night after night with our infant son, no idea where her husband was. And of course, I wasn't about to tell her what I'd been up to. I went straight into our bedroom and fell into bed, only coming out late in the afternoon to demand my tea.

In those days, I hadn't the least regard for Christine. I refused to settle down to the role of husband, provider, friend. I lived from day to day like a predator: I was on the make for easy sex, easy money and easy targets. My wife was my property, my slave.

This was my life for the three years we lived together under the same roof. It amazes me as I consider my life then how Christine could have stayed with me. I was on a massive ego trip. I was young and I felt immortal. I never once worried that my lifestyle put Christine at risk, even though she was in greater need of my love and support than at any time in our lives since we had been together.

After Christopher was born, I must have been affected by some latent paternal instinct, because it was then that I broke off with my terrorist career. I put it to some of the men whom I was under that I wanted a total break from active duty. Remarkably, there was no pressure put on me as a result of this decision. I felt as though I'd managed to disentangle myself from the web of deceit, murder and debauchery which entangled my life. Little did I know then that within a few short months after Smith's death I'd be behind bars on fifty-eight separate charges under Northern Ireland's Prevention of Terrorism Act—all as the result of a murder that I hadn't committed.

# Chapter Eight

It was the morning of 17th September 1980. As I lay in bed next to Christine, I heard a knock at the front door of our flat. Stirring, I glanced at the alarm clock on the stand next to the bed. Six o'clock. I groaned inwardly. 'Who could that be?' I said to Christine, but she was still asleep.

As I padded along the corridor to answer the door, I became aware of a sick feeling in the pit of my stomach. Pausing, I pressed my ear to the door and strained to listen for a clue. There was only the sound of my pulse beating inside my head. 'Who's there?' I finally called through the door.

'Police. May we come in?'

'Certainly,' I said, playing it cool. 'What's wrong?' I asked, swinging the door open.

There stood a plain clothes officer and two others in uniform. The first one proffered his identification. 'Do you object to us searching the flat?' he said in a flat tone.

'No, help yourselves, officer,' I replied.

'Billy, what is it?' called Christine from the bedroom.

'My wife's in there,' was all I could think to say.

The police made a thorough search of the rooms, looking no doubt for guns or other evidence of my terrorist activities.

I stood aside and watched. The men were efficient and looked as though they were working according to a pattern. No doubt they knew what they were looking for.

Despite their combing the whole of the flat without missing a corner, nothing was found, so I thought I was in the clear. 'I'm sure there must have been some mistake,' I offered in a jovial manner. They made no reply. I stepped over to the door and was just about to show the police out when one of them said, 'Get your clothes on, McFetridge. You're coming with us.'

'You can't do that; you don't have a warrant.'

The plain clothes man produced a document and said, 'You're under arrest for murder. Now get dressed.'

I looked closely at the paper to be certain there was no mistake. I swallowed hard. It was signed by the Secretary of State for Northern Ireland. I shrugged and returned to the bedroom where Christine cowered. I don't know who she was more afraid of: me or the police. Up until now, she never knew for certain that I was a terrorist, let alone a murderer.

'They want me to go with them,' I said to Christine. She said nothing as I fumbled with my clothing and shoes.

As I dressed, my mind worked frantically. How had it happened? I'd never once been arrested nor implicated in a crime.

Summoning up all my self-assurance as I was led out of the flat in handcuffs, I called over my shoulder to Christine, 'Call our solicitor. And for heaven's sake, don't worry. I'll be back in a couple of hours.' In fact, it would be seven years before I'd be free. And by then Christine and our baby, Christopher, would be gone from my life for good.

It was a cool, wet morning and the irony of the drive down to Castlereagh in Belfast crashed upon me like a cold Atlantic breaker. Whereas the last time I had driven into Belfast I was a powerful man in charge of my life, able to decide who would live or die; on that morning it was I who was a captive bird held by others who would make all the major decisions in my life for me. My visions of self-grandeur faded, and all I could do was hope that the charge wouldn't stick.

At the police station, I discovered that my arrest went back to the death of Smith a few months earlier. The night the police ran a check on me at the road block, several years of suspicion came to fruition. I had been watched for months, but there was never any substantial evidence to link me with even a traffic violation, let alone terrorist acts. It was mere suspicion until the night of 10th June 1980. Since I was working at the scene of Smith's death and had known connections with the UDA, the police at last had a reason to take me in.

Even before we reached the interrogation centre, I'd decided to play it tough and stonewall all of their questions. At least I knew that Smith's was one murder I hadn't committed.

Three officers were assigned to interview me. The room where I was questioned was small and nondescript. Glancing about me, I saw there were no windows. The light was harsh and the air was still and smelled of perspiration.

When the interrogation began, I kept a steady

gaze into the cops' eyes but said nothing in response to the questions they threw at me.

'You're a tough one, eh, McFetridge?' rasped one of the officers after a few minutes.

'Yeah,' I replied. 'The problem is you have the wrong man!'

'Oh? And who do you think we should have in here?'

I nearly had to bite my lip from being tricked into naming names like that, so I said nothing.

'Yeah, real tough, when the victim hasn't a snowball's chance in hell of getting away,' my interrogator mocked.

From behind me someone slapped my head. It didn't hurt, but it shook me up some.

'Let me just read you a list of crimes we know you've played a part in,' said the first officer. To my chagrin, most of the charges were accurate, but one of the charges the police had laid against me was false—Smith's death. Of all the charges, this was the most serious. Was I being framed?

'Well, Billy? What do you have to say for yourself?'

If I protested that one charge was inaccurate, that would be the same as admitting that the others were true. But if I didn't protest, I'd be set up for life without a doubt. My mind felt thick and I found it hard to think straight. The last thing I wanted to do was to confess to a crime I'd not committed. For the time being I decided to keep my mouth shut.

The officers looked at me as the first one said, 'We have all the time in the world, McFetridge. Time is on our side, you might say.'

The hours passed by, and still they fired questions at me. I longed for a cup of tea and a break. I wanted to get up and walk about. Still the unending barrage of questions continued. At last I was sent back to my holding cell until the next day, and the next, and the next, as the whole process was painstakingly repeated.

As the days passed, the police came to the interrogations fresh and well fed. I, on the other hand, was a nervous wreck. I hadn't been eating or sleeping well. I also had a hard time keeping my alibis straight from day to day. I began to contradict myself. I couldn't distinguish what was true and what wasn't. I felt like I was on drugs. By the end of the week my guilt was obvious.

'Come on, lad,' crooned an officer. 'Sign here and that'll put an end to all this questioning.' He proffered a pen. I took it in my hand, hesitated, then scrawled my name on the official form.

In my confused state, and as the result of the mental and physical duress under which I was placed, I confessed to all charges, including Smith's murder—the one crime I'd never committed. But for some strange reason it didn't matter to me any more. At that stage, all I wanted was to get away from my interrogators and their endless questions. I reasoned that the sooner I signed their confession forms, the sooner I could get away for some food and a decent sleep. I didn't know then that this error of judgement would come back to haunt me in the months ahead.

Once my confession was a *fait accompli*, I was ordered to follow a sombre police officer. In silence we descended two floors until we were in the basement. The dank air smelled of carbolic acid.

'Get your clothes off, McFetridge,' commanded the police guard. I made a half-hearted start until I met his hard stony stare. He obviously meant business. I didn't like to undress before anyone, but I had no choice. Off came my shoes and socks; my shirt and vest; my trousers and pants. I stood naked and defenceless, like a child awaiting my next order.

Then with a nod of his head he added, 'Step into that tub.'

Lifting one foot and poking it gingerly into the hot water, I was unprepared for what happened next. Shoving a stiff brush into my hands, the guard ordered me to scrub every part of my body, even my private parts.

My mind reeled with indignation while the guard watched me scrub myself down with a brush and carbolic soap. Once the bath was over, the humiliation didn't end: 'Get over there and lean on the wall with your hands and legs apart.' I obeyed and grimaced while this man checked carefully for tattoos and other distinguishing marks on my body. He even checked under my scrotum and in my anus. I felt angry because to me I was being treated like an animal, not a person. He was stealing my identity. All I was to this man was horse flesh to be processed and passed along to the next point on an assembly line of nameless, faceless men.

Once this ordeal had ended I was allowed to dress in a prison uniform, and sent off to meet the head of the prison.

'We run a tight ship around here, McFetridge,' said the governor of Belfast Prison, barely meeting my eye as he read out the conditions of my stay in his prison. 'You, of course, have your rights, but—and this is an important but—we have our rules. Keep out of trouble and mind your step, and you'll find your time here to be reasonably pleasant. Get out of line, and we'll step on you fast and hard.' He was severe and laid down the law in no uncertain terms.

While in remand, I shared a ten feet by eight feet

cell with another man. There were two beds, a chamber pot, a bookshelf and a chair. Although there was a barred window which could be opened a few inches, the cell was very warm. Another thing I recall about that cell, and all other cells I occupied, was the constant noise coming from somewhere. Sometimes it was a loud *thump, thump, thump*; more often it was a low, hardly audible, *tic, tic, tic*. I was to live like a goldfish in a warm world of constant noise.

That day I knew it was all over for me—possibly for many, many years. Did I make any political statements such as, 'I did this all in the name of a free Ulster', or, 'You may have got me, but there are a score more just waiting to take my place'? You know, the kind of thing one might see in a Hollywood film. I said nothing of the kind.

How did I feel? I wasn't angry. I wasn't scared. The unvarnished truth is that I felt an over-whelming sense of relief. It was finally all over. I had lived for nearly seven years with the spectre that one day I would be caught or killed. That ghost had been exorcised. In a way, this was a severe mercy. I had lost my freedom, but I had retained my life.

Did I have any regrets? Yes. I regretted having joined the UDA. But this was part and parcel of what I was; what I had become. When the net came down, I thought no more about my political aspirations.

On the face of it, capture was streets better than being killed. I felt no cause was worth dying for, least of all the cause of terrorism. Since I was still alive, I had to make a go of the rest of my life. Of course, I was fearful of the new episode that I was about to enter.

The only truly friendly person to speak to me

during my remand was the prison chaplain. He turned up at my cell one morning and peered inside the window at me as I sat morosely on my bed. Clearing his throat, he introduced himself. I mumbled something back without looking at him.

'Where're you from, Billy?' I looked at him in surprise. He didn't ask me about my crimes. Until then, I never expected anyone to care about the other factors of the life I had left behind me. I had to think for a moment in order to recall the answer to this perfectly ordinary question asked under extraordinary circumstances. 'I'm from Larne,' I replied. Normally, I'd never have given a clergyman the time of day. Nevertheless, it occurred to me that I was grateful for the time the chaplain gave me. My whole life, I'd been too busy doing my own thing to be grateful to anyone, even for the big things such as the breaks given to me by my commanding officer in the army; the love of my wife and family. Now a simple conversation and a friendly face meant the whole world to me. Loss of freedom was forcing me to rethink my whole value system.

At home in Larne, Christine was shocked and full of questions—questions which she and the rest of my family had purposely not asked me over the years. They had turned a blind eye to my late night comings and goings. Only once had anyone in my family asked me what I was up to. That was my mother. And my cynical reply was, 'Ask me no questions, and I'll tell you no lies.'

My wife's greatest fear was for Christopher. My words, 'I'm sorry' rang hollow in her ears. And while I was dreadfully sorry for my family and loved ones, the events of the next few months proved that I was sorrier still for myself. My hardest lessons were all still in the future.

# Chapter Nine

As days drifted into weeks and months, I had time
to reflect on the mess I'd made of my life. I felt grief
for what I had done to my marriage. Izaak Walton
once wrote that no man can lose what he never had,
but upon reflection I began to see that Christine and
I had indeed had something, and my loss was acute.
While ours was not a perfect marriage, we did have
the basis of a relationship. It was far from a perfect
relationship. Christine was the giver and I was the
taker. But now what little we did have was fast
fading.

To cope with the mental anguish I faced, I
decided to try to live for the future. What inspired
me to adopt this stoic attitude was the fact that I
knew that one day I would be free to take off my
drab prison uniform and walk out of the front gates
and begin my life again. Naturally, I assumed my
wife and son would wait for me.

At the time of my arrest, September 1980, my son
was about eighteen months old, and Christine was
still a considerable part of my life. For the first year

or so of my imprisonment, Christine coped as best she could with other people's probing questions. While I was behind bars, I had lost my identity: I was merely a number. But out in the real world Christine had lost her identity too; out there she was now reduced to being Billy's wife.

To this day I have nothing but admiration for her because of her loyalty. It was I who landed in trouble and who made her life hell. Christine loved me, but I had refused to remain faithful to her. I've already said that over the years I'd never learned to be grateful to anyone—not to my mother and her unconditional love; not to my taciturn father who worked to provide me with a decent home, clean clothes and food in my belly; not to my commanding officers who could have had the book thrown at me and then dishonourably discharged me from the army; and not even to Christine who affirmed my masculinity, who cooked my meals, and who bore me a healthy son. Now the circumstances had been radically changed, and I became entirely dependent on her visits for moral support. And she offered it unselfishly.

I was still ungrateful. It's not that I didn't want to be grateful. I wanted to change my life and be like a Hollywood prisoner who learns his lesson and who decides to reform. I found that my behaviour disgusted even me. I wasn't free to change my selfish ways.

If I had been a swine to my wife as a free man, I was perhaps an even worse one behind bars. You see, even as a prisoner, I just naturally expected Christine to run back and forth from the prison responding to my every request week after week.

During the times when Christine came along to

visit me, I never stopped griping about my needs, or how badly I was being treated. From the moment she made an appearance I'd confront her with gripes. I complained about everything: the food was stinking, I wasn't getting enough exercise, I still hadn't seen a doctor or dentist, they brought us in early from the exercise yard, the screws were giving me a hard time. For the whole thirty minutes it was always me, me, me. I barely left time for Christine to get a word in edgeways about her needs, her complaints or those of our son.

One day I had been pouring out my usual litany of grievances right up to the time when Christine had to leave. The guard who was standing nearby waited until she had gone before he stepped up to me and tapped me on the shoulder. I turned and fixed him with a dirty look as he said, 'Do you guys ever think just what your wives have to go through running up here week in, week out, for years on end, just because you need new training shoes, new jeans or whatever? And yet she's trying to run a house and raise a boy on little or no money.'

My scowl remained fixed, but as his words got under my skin, I realised he was right. He continued, 'You expect her to run here and there, bringing you newspapers and magazines. And yet it's she who needs help. In here you lot have everything laid on for you. This lady has to run a home outside! Think about that, McFetridge!'

I was all set to make a smart remark, but my quip wouldn't come. From the sincere tone of his voice and the veracity of his words, I stood there as a twice condemned man. I couldn't make a defence. From that day I resolved to stop thinking about myself.

The very next week, I began to talk to Christine

about her needs and those of Christopher; anything but my own filthy little list of complaints. It wasn't easy, but the words of that guard rang in my mind and helped me to become a sympathetic listener to my wife.

People may not realise it, but the wives of prisoners are every bit as imprisoned as the ones in the cells. The wives are prisoners of frustration, loneliness and heartbreak. Their twenty-four-hour-a-day guards are not uniformed officers with keys; they are guards called fear and uncertainty. They remain 'on duty' even when the wives are asleep.

Things remained hard for Christine, despite my attempts at being sociable. But I think the small change encouraged her to hope that perhaps there might be some future for our marriage.

To that end, she came up with an idea which was meant to help our relationship. Although neither of us were especially religious, she wanted us to have our marriage blessed in a special service. Basically, what she planned to do was to have us retake our marriage vows before the prison chaplain.

At first I was unsure about this, but upon reflection I agreed. For one thing, what did I have to lose? If it could help our situation, then I was willing to do almost anything she requested. And another thing, I had been shown a small kindness by the chaplain, so I felt I could trust him to help me with my crumbling marriage.

I made an appointment with the padre and nervously explained my request.

'I think this is a wise thing to do, Billy,' he said with a warm smile. He went on to explain, 'All this ceremony will involve is your repeating the marriage vows. This way the two of you will reassure

each other of the love that is the bond of this union.'
I smiled and shrugged, saying, 'Let's go for it.'

We were given a New Testament by the chaplain,
and although I had been an unfaithful husband as a
free man, I now resolved to honour my vows. One
might point out cynically that it was the bars which
prevented my philandering, but in looking back I
now know I had taken the first step on the road to
repentance and reconciliation—with my wife, with
God and with my former enemies, the IRA.

On the day, I felt as nervous as on our first
wedding day. I paced my cell until it was time to go.
Although I didn't wear special clothing, I felt every
bit as grand in my prison uniform as if I'd worn a
top hat and tails. The service was over in a few
minutes, and after taking Christine in my arms and
kissing her goodbye, I made my way back to my
grotty little cell instead of speeding off with my
blushing bride to enjoy God's wonderful gifts of love
and sex.

I'm sure that this simple ceremony was blessed by
God, and it was probably that which kept our
marriage together for the next five years.

Despite my brushes with religion, I still had no
genuine interest in God (other than how religion
might be useful to me while I was a prisoner). I
certainly knew nothing of Jesus Christ nor his love
for me. Christianity remained for me a set of rules
and regulations, duties and obligations. But time
was rapidly running out, and before long Jesus
would come into the prison and turn around my life
a full 180 degrees.

# Chapter Ten

One thing about life in prison, it gives a person plenty of time to think. Before too long, I began to think about the meaning of life. We all need something in which we can believe.

As a young man, I chose hedonism—eat, drink and be merry, for tomorrow you die—but before long I learned that this selfish road is a lonely one on which to travel. Hedonism doesn't meet the need for meaningful human contact.

Later, I chose the Loyalist cause in Northern Ireland, thinking that here was a cause greater than myself, a cause rife with dignity, purpose and self-sacrifice. In less than a decade, however, I came to see nationalism of any sort as a sham and a vile deception.

Even my marriage was coming undone, despite the vows that Christine and I had retaken, saying we would love and honour each other. Was anything real? Was there anything worth living for? This was truly the lowest point of my life, and that's when God came in.

After being in the Crumlin Road Prison in Belfast for a few months, I learned that Christianity is not merely a religion. Rather it is a powerful way of life, and it exists inside prisons as well as outside.

Case in point: one day a prison officer came by and invited me to come to a Bible study. I saw this as an ideal chance to get out of my cell for an extra hour or so a week, so I said I would like to come along.

I went to a small Bible study led by the late Rev Bill Vance, a very godly man who had served God in the prisons of Northern Ireland most of his life. Over the years he led countless offenders to salvation in the Lord Jesus Christ.

Bill made an effort to get to know us prisoners. I could tell he had our interests at heart, and that he respected us despite our being behind bars. Because of this, prisoners were naturally drawn to Bill.

What's more, Bill talked about the Bible *as if everything were true*. To him, the Scriptures were as real as the morning's headlines. This was no pansy, this was a man's man. Through him, I came to learn that Jesus was real too—and not in merely the historic sense of real. Jesus was around today, and every bit as interested in the affairs of men in modern Ulster as he was in ancient Palestine. To say this was a radical revelation would be an understatement.

After a few months, I found that I was able to open up to Bill. Although I wasn't used to talking about my innermost emotions, fears and concerns, I found Bill was easy to talk to. He listened and seemed to understand me.

We talked about prayer, and before long I can honestly say that my prayers stopped being cries into the darkness. Bill showed me that God was real, and he was there listening to me when I spoke to him. Moreover, God replied to anyone who called to him. For the first time ever, my prayers became two-way conversations with God. Of course I never heard God's voice with my ears, but I couldn't deny that he spoke to me in my mind, through certain situations and even other people—and not just prison chaplains.

Not long after, as I was crossing the Crumlin Road to the court for a remand hearing, I was joined by a fellow prisoner called Bobby. By the time we were both in the holding cell, we got to talking about our families. I began to moan about the way I felt, the way my friends had all abandoned me—the usual litany. I must have seemed pathetic to Bobby, because when I had finished complaining about life, instead of joining in the gripe session, he challenged me. 'You know,' he said, 'despite all of our problems, and the fact that our families and friends might not stick by us, there's still one person who cares very much for us.'

'Who's that?' I snapped.

'The Lord,' he replied.

*Oh no*, I thought, *another Christian*.

'We're here because we did wrong. We have to pay the price. But God loves you, Billy.'

Bobby's words were simple, and in any other circumstances I would have disregarded them as so much pious talk. But in the starkness of confinement, in a place where there was none who really loved me, his words sank deeply into my mind. I knew God was speaking to me. This time God used a fellow prisoner who was as bad as I was—or had once been—since he was behind bars too. Another thunderbolt from heaven came crashing my way: vicars and pastors aren't the only ones God uses to communicate his love to his children. He can even use a crooked stick like Bobby to draw a straight line.

From that day forward, I began listening regularly for God to speak. That's when the Bible came alive to me. I started to read the Bible instead of the newspaper or trashy novels. I was gobsmacked by what God revealed to me through those flimsy pages.

Previously, I had felt that the Bible was full of does and don'ts. By taking time to read carefully and systematically, I saw that it was just the opposite. The Bible was a road map showing the best options made accessible to us by God through his Son's death and resurrection.

The best revelation was that, far from being disgusted by me because of my sins, Jesus was crazy about me. That's why he died for me. But why did he have to die? Couldn't he just have said, 'All is forgiven,' and spared himself the indignity of capital punishment Roman style?

The Bible says that the wages of sin is death (Romans 6:23). That means if you sin, you die: physically as well as spiritually. Jesus loved me so much that he was willing to die in my place so that I wouldn't have to be punished for my sins. This is a concept any prisoner will be able to relate to precisely because which of us prisoners hasn't at one time or another longed for a bloke to come along and trade places with us, no questions asked? This was what Jesus had always wanted to do for me, only I'd always been too busy running my own affairs to respond to God's love.

Step one in my conversion was embracing the love of God. One passage which came alive to me from the Bible was John 3:16: 'For God so loved the world that he gave his one and only Son, that whoever believes in him shall not perish but have eternal life.' I who had been starved of love for so many years responded to this statement of fact like a flower responds to rain.

Later on, I told Bobby how amazed I was to realise that Jesus loved me. Bobby only chuckled. I could tell he knew exactly what this revelation meant to me. It was as if he was saying, 'I know, Billy. It was the same for me.'

A passage which remained for me to come to terms with was John 3:3, where it says that unless a man is born again, he cannot enter into the kingdom of God. For me as a prisoner, I could understand the need for rebirth. It was what I longed for; indeed, what the State had put me in jail for. Over the months, I'd tried under my own power to become a new man. I'd been able to reprogramme certain aspects of my personality, but not all of them. At the end of the day I was still a corrupt man with no power to change my selfish ways.

Bill Vance once said that no man can reinvent himself. Only God can do that for us, and the Bible calls it being 'born again'.

'You must ask God to cause it to happen,' Bill told me. 'Then you must believe it is so. Soon you will see that you are a new creature. Even if the changes are gradual, they will be real.'

Quietly and alone one night in March 1981, I knelt in my cell in the Crumlin Road Prison, and invited Jesus into my heart to become my Saviour and Lord. I wanted to be born again, saved from the wages of my own sins.

My prayer was rambling and incoherent, but I asked Jesus into my life to become my Saviour and Lord. I placed my life and future under his control as it says in 1 Peter 3:15: '. . . have reverence for Christ in your hearts, and honour him as Lord' (Good News Bible).

By doing this I had become united with Christ who gave me an entirely new start in life that night: 'Therefore, if anyone is in Christ, he is a new creation; the old has gone, the new has come' (2 Corinthians 5:17). There were no bells, nor were there any rockets going off, when I had done it. It was much better than that. A quiet feeling of peace crested over my whole being like a gentle wave of the sea. For the first time ever, I felt one with God and with the universe, despite my being locked up in a cell miles from loved ones and the comforts of home.

In September of 1981 I was charged officially with my crimes. It was then, nearly a year after I had made my initial confession, that my having admitted to Smith's murder came back to haunt me with a vengeance. Until then, I had not thought about this serious error I'd made. Now I was completely dumbfounded and horrified to hear that the police were planning to use this charge to put me away for good. 'Why on earth did I ever confess to a crime I hadn't committed?' I wailed as I paced around my tiny cell.

Facing the prospect of this last charge, I knew that this one crime would be the test of whether or not I trusted that God had my best interests at heart. Despite my anguish, I slipped down on my knees and prayed simply, 'I commit this whole mess into your hands, Father. Thy will be done. Amen.'

Soon after, a woman prison visitor called Agnes Hancock paid a call to my cell. I confided my situation to Agnes, who then shared my needs with some of her prayer partners outside of the prison.

Agnes turned out to be a beautiful Christian woman with a remarkable story of her own. She was very good to me while I was behind bars, and I found that in the times when I was really struggling to find faith, Agnes would turn up or I'd receive a letter from her. These small kindnesses may not seem much to you, but to a man in prison awaiting a certain life sentence, such contact is a lifeline.

One day I was agonising over my having signed that wretched confession. Sure as clockwork, Agnes came to me and said, 'If you are innocent of this particular charge, then God will not allow you to be punished for it.' What struck me about the old woman's words was that they were spoken more like a prophecy than as mere words of condolence.

As the trial began, the authorities were adamant that the murder charge should stick. They had a signed confession. It would take nothing short of a miracle now to save me from being wrongly charged with a crime I'd not committed.

My defence fought well on my behalf in the courtroom, but privately my legal advisors were preparing me for the worst. One solicitor had said to me, 'The police have their piece of paper with your signature on it. That means this is an open and shut case. You never should have signed that confession, Billy. Don't be surprised if you go down for life.' My heart sank at his words.

During one morning of the third week of my trial, I was feeling especially downcast, despite Agnes' prophecy and the support of a network of prayer across Ulster on my behalf. My heart sank even more when I met with my barrister in a downstairs room before the day's proceedings began. His face seemed to be hiding something as he sat down opposite me. I feared the worst.

'Billy, I have some important news for you.'

I waited to hear his words, fully expecting him to tell me that he and his colleagues had thrown in the towel.

'I had a telephone call this morning from the Department of Public Prosecution, and they informed me that in relation to your particular case, they would be prepared to drop the murder charge.'

I was shocked. I was too stunned to speak.

'Well, Billy? Are you relieved? It's just possible you won't be going to prison for life.'

'Of course I'm relieved. This is great news.'

But my barrister put up his hand. 'There's one caveat, Billy. The deal is that they will drop the murder charge provided you'll plead guilty to manslaughter.'

'They've got a deal,' I retorted. I didn't have to think twice about it. My feet hardly touched the steps as I ascended the stairs to the courtroom.

My guilty plea was accepted and at the end of my trial I was charged with fifty-eight offences under the Prevention of Terrorism Act, including the following:

Count 1 (manslaughter): twelve years' imprisonment.

Counts 2–6 (accomplice to murder): eight years' imprisonment on each count.

Counts 15–17 & 21 (robbery, Larne Football Club): ten years' imprisonment on each count.

Count 23 (armed resistance to arrest, robbery,

possession of deadly firearms): twelve years' imprisonment.

Counts 25–27 (fire bombings): seven years' imprisonment on each count.

Counts 28–32, 34, 36, 38–39 (pipe bombings): five years' imprisonment on each count.

Count 58 (possession of seven hand guns, one sub-machine gun, one rifle, two zip guns, and a quantity of ammunition): six years' imprisonment.

The total number of years to which I was sentenced came to 152 years. However, due to my plea bargaining, I was to serve only twelve years' imprisonment on the manslaughter charge. The remaining counts would be concurrent.

Now you might think that I immediately fell on my knees and thanked God that Agnes' prophecy had come about, but in fact I didn't. I was too caught up with other matters. I was also a very new Christian at the time, so my thinking was still conditioned by my years of ingratitude. Fortunately, my thinking was to change for the better in the very near future, but the changes wouldn't be fast, nor would they be easy.

# Chapter Eleven

Prison is a totally different society from that of the outside. In prison everybody minds his own business. The first rule is: you do not ask another prisoner why he's there. In time it may or may not come out, but it's entirely up to that person to divulge the information when and how he likes.

I came across all kinds of different people during my years in various Ulster prisons. I learned very quickly how to analyse other people. Before long, I was categorising people, putting labels on them for my own reference. This way I knew which ones to stay clear of (the rapists and sex offenders) and which ones to associate with (the politicals and white-collar criminals). At the end of the day, such knowledge helps a prisoner to survive.

Many times a prisoner feels completely hopeless. His whole life is in the hands of somebody else who makes all his decisions. Therefore it's not surprising that at some point a prisoner will begin to contemplate suicide.

There was one such man whom I'll call Mick.

When I knew him he was in remand, and it was likely he'd be put away for a long stretch. His cell was the one next to mine, so we had opportunities to chat to one another. One day he asked me if I was married.

'Yeah, Mick,' I said, not wanting to volunteer much more than that. Yet I could tell from his eyes that he wanted to talk, so I asked if he was married.

Nodding vigorously, he said, 'Yes, I just got married. But I'm going crazy because she'll probably be sleeping around with my mates. She'll probably leave me while I rot in here.'

His yellowed eyes darted around. He looked to me like a rat searching for an escape tunnel.

I reached for a cigarette and offered him one. 'Relax,' I said. 'Take it easy.' I didn't like the crazed look of fear in his eyes. I thought a fag would calm him down.

Mick refused the cigarette and turned and walked away. I shook my head and made a note to stay away from Mick. If I paid attention to what he was saying, I'd become a nervous wreck as well. Prison is not the place for emotional outbursts.

That night Mick decided to kill himself.

Just before the lights went out, Mick looked over at his eighteen-year-old cell mate and said, 'I'm going to cut my wrists. You just mind your own business. Do you understand?'

Thinking Mick was bluffing, his mate snorted, 'Sure thing, Mick. See you in the mornin'.' He then rolled over on his side and closed his eyes. It was when he heard the smashing of a glass and a sharp gasp that he realised Mick might have been serious.

The young man opened his eyes and saw Mick calmly holding his profusely bleeding left wrist over a large enamel tea cup. The blood squirted out in jets.

Lunging for the emergency alarm bell inside the cell, the boy stopped short when Mick called out, 'Touch that ****ing bell and I'll have just enough time to slice your neck from ear lobe to ear lobe.' Mick held up the shard of bloody glass and shook it menacingly.

'Mick. . .'

'You just climb back into your bed and mind your own business, laddie, and let me mind mine. I'm not going to rot in this cell, and neither you nor anyone else is going to make me rot here.'

Shaking and confused, the boy blinked back his tears and lay on his bed with his face to the wall while Mick stood up and seized the tea cup. He began to splash blood all over the walls, floor and ceiling of the small cell. It was his final futile act of outraged defiance. Soon the air was thick with the odour of fresh blood and Mick, feeling faint, fell back onto his bed, panting, waiting for death to come.

I was asleep in the next cell when my slumber was disturbed by frantic voices coming from next door. The hourly check was underway when the guard had looked in and seen the blood and Mick's ghastly white face. 'Hey, what's going on in there?' he demanded. Mick's eyes flickered slightly. The boy rolled over and cried out, 'He's sliced his wrist!'

Since the keys were kept off the wing, the guard fumbled for his radio and called for assistance to open the cell door. He could see that every second mattered if Mick's life was to be saved.

Within minutes the wail of an ambulance filled the night air, and frantic footsteps rang out from the metal stairs leading up to our landing.

Overcome by curiosity, I stood and peered out of the flap in my door and flinched when I saw two ambulance men removing a prone body from the cell next to mine. At first I couldn't make out who it was. All I saw was a horribly limp arm dangling and a trail of bloody footprints all over the floor. Then as they passed my cell I saw Mick's face. His blue lips were parted exposing a grey tongue, and his eyes were glazed over and unseeing. I turned away in disgust and tumbled back into bed.

The whole episode ended as quickly as it began, but I couldn't go back to sleep. I lay awake on my bed for hours, unable to rest as I recalled the haunted look of panic in Mick's eyes earlier in the day. *Still*, I thought, *perhaps that poor bastard's better off now*. With this thought uppermost in my mind, I turned onto my side and eventually drifted off to sleep.

The next day, the guards took all of us on the wing one by one to see the bloody walls and ceiling of Mick's cell. The place smelled like a butcher's shop; dried blood literally covered the ceilings and walls. The guard told us all the gory details of the suicide attempt in a flat, unemotional voice. I suppose the idea was to put us off trying anything so rash ourselves. Fortunately for Mick, the hospital is right next to the prison and his death was just averted. When Mick was finally released from hospital, he was sent to a psychiatric ward to do his time.

I didn't need the guard's vivid object lesson to keep me from attempting suicide. I had no urge to do myself in. One thing which my life as a soldier and then as a terrorist had taught me was that survival is the most important instinct of all.

The thing I feared most of all during my time in prison was being raped.

During all my time in prison I only came across a single incident of male on male rape. One night after lights out, a succession of terrifying screams began to echo up and down the wing. I can't say why or how I knew it, but it was so obvious to me that it was a rape. At first I thought the guards would soon be on the scene, so I lay awake listening. The longer I listened, the more I was able to follow what was happening. I won't go into the details; they are too revolting to repeat.

As the screams continued, I was up on my feet wondering when the guards would arrive. But they never did come. The terrifying pleas for mercy and shouts of pain continued until all that could be heard were the muffled sobs of a degraded human being. I felt as if I'd vomit any moment if I allowed myself to think too deeply about what had just taken place, so I pushed it to the back of my mind and lay down on my bed and went back to sleep.

In the morning, word got out that somehow a seasoned sex offender had been assigned a teenaged cell mate and as soon as the lights went out, the older man was upon his prey. How such a match could have been made, or why the guards didn't intervene that time, I cannot say. To this day the pitiful pleas of that boy still echo in my mind.

Later, in 1981, a general outbreak of unrest occurred in my sector, A-Wing, of the Crumlin Road Prison. It was due to acute overcrowding in the prison. A-Wing of the prison was taken over by inmates for nearly a week.

At the start, the prison authorities sealed off our wing, but instead of making a physical assault on us, the decision was made to starve and freeze us out.

To that end the heating was turned off and water

guns were used to douse anyone who tried to scale out onto the roof.

Soon furniture was being broken up and fires were made, not so much in protest, but to keep warm. A few of the hardiest men managed to climb onto the roof-tops, wet, cold and hungry. From their perches on the roof, they were able to give interviews to the media which spelled out the men's grievances.

About four days into the protest, a leader of the protest came to me and ordered me to climb out onto the roof to relieve one of the men out there.

Until this happened, I was able to remain aloof in my unlocked cell. But now I had to make a decision.

Once before I'd allowed other men to do my thinking for me when I was with the paramilitaries. Now, years later, I was learning to muster the courage of my convictions; to say 'no' instead of knuckle under to peer pressure. All of us suffered from the conditions in the prison, so I was with the other men on that score. But I wanted to reform it, not fight it.

'There's no way I'm going up there. I'm a Christian and I don't agree with using violence to attain our goals—even goals which I wholeheartedly support.'

The man's face turned red and I braced myself for his vitriolic tirade, but instead this man replied, 'OK, lad. I won't force you to go up there. But if that's the way you want it, then I'll have to lock you up.'

I shrugged and said, 'I don't mind. All I want now is to do my time and get out of here, back to my family.' I was led away and put in a cell by myself. Within hours, the cell began to fill up with more and more men who refused to support the riot. Apparently, word had got around that I had stood up to the ring leaders, and others were following my example.

In a day or two, a large group of men who had refused to support their fellow inmates in the takeover of the wing had assembled. To my delight, many in this group were Christians. I waited to see what the Lord might have to say to us as the riot continued to rage all around us.

By now more men had climbed up onto the roof, and any food which was found was sent up to them.

By the end of the week it was clear that the protest was a stalemate, so word was sent out to set A-Wing on fire. I knew this was a crazy idea, but there was nothing I or anyone else could do. As far as I could see, the riot was now totally out of control.

One young lad began to scream, 'If they set fire to the place the ****ing roof will collapse on us. None of us'll get out of here alive!'

At his hysterical words, the atmosphere in the cell tensed up.

Another man called out, 'We'll fry unless we can bust out!'

Several of the men began quite literally to try to dig their way out of the walls using parts of beds, knives or anything hard which they could lay their hands on. Others pushed against the bars of the cell. If something wasn't done, and quickly, I feared that the men would begin to tear each other apart in their attempt to escape roasting alive. The big question was: what could be done?

The rest of the lads looked to me for their lead. By this time, I felt that the Lord was telling me to get the men to pray. I was very reluctant to suggest we pray about the problem in the light of the general mayhem which surrounded us. After all, what good could praying do when we were facing the prospect of being burned alive? But I recalled all that had happened to me in the last few months, and decided that God knew better than I what was to be done.

Clearing my throat I spoke up softly, 'I think we should put this whole situation into God's hands. We need to pray, and pray now.' Was this really me suggesting that we kneel and pray? I could hardly believe the change which had come over me in the last few months. The oddest thing was that even as I spoke to the men my panic gave way to a sense of conviction.

I dropped onto my knees and prayed, 'Heavenly Father, we give you praise for this opportunity for you to demonstrate your authority even over the Crumlin Road Prison. Thank you that you are our God and that we may rest in your goodness.

'Lord, we hand this prison over to you. We ask you to watch over us in this cell. We ask that not one hair of our heads be touched by the flames. But not our will but yours, Lord Jesus. Amen.'

My sense of peace must have been contagious, because the whole cell full of caged and frantic men became calm, even though we could hear the destruction going on outside of the prison. Time crept by and the dreaded blaze never materialised. I later learned that several fires were indeed started in the roof space, but they went out before they could affect the whole wing. Answered prayer? I say it was. But the prayers affected more than the fires.

Just as the riot had reached a fever pitch, the prison authorities came forward and offered an amnesty for the prisoners if they agreed to call off the protest. The leaders agreed to this face-saving plan, and the riot ended as quickly as it had begun.

Few of us had eaten a bite of food in five or six days, so we were glad to be rounded up and taken to a different wing for as much soup and boiled potatoes as we could eat. I never tasted a meal so satisfying!

That night, I was thinking of the words of the 121st Psalm: 'The Lord watches over you—the Lord is your shade at your right hand . . . The Lord will keep you from all harm—he will watch over your life; the Lord will watch over your coming and going both now and for evermore' (Ps 121:5, 7–8).

'It's true!' I cried out. 'The Lord really does have our lives in his hands!'

Although I didn't know what the future held for me, I knew then and there that as long as I was faithful to God, he would be my security and my constant companion. That night I rolled over and slept the soundest and most peaceful sleep of my life. From then on, I needn't worry about being the captain of my life. I had relinquished this to God. My job from that day on was simply to be faithful.

# Chapter Twelve

As a result of the extensive damage caused to A-Wing of Crumlin Road Prison, it was decided that we would be moved to the Maze Prison. Personally, I was excited about the move. For one thing, I'd heard that living conditions there were generally better than what I'd been used to. Also, I looked forward to a change of scenery.

After I had settled into a regular pattern in the H-block of the Maze Prison, I found time to reflect on the full implication of what it meant when I had given my life over to Jesus. For the first time since my trial and sentencing, I was able to see clearly how God had been with me in the months leading up to this very moment.

There is a verse in the 1662 Prayer Book which goes, 'The Lord looseth men out of prison: the Lord giveth sight to the blind,' and this was to become a guiding principle in my life.

After the excitement of my trial and sentencing had worn off, the reality of having to spend twelve years of my life caged up as an animal in Ulster's grimmest prison might have worn me down. But it didn't. In fact, even though I'd forgotten about God in the aftermath of my trial and the move to the Maze, he hadn't forgotten about me.

Now that I knew my fate, as it were, I had time to put the sequence of my life into an eternal perspective. It was no coincidence that I met so many Christians at so critical a time in my life. But was Christianity merely a psychological crutch, or was there really a supernatural power behind all the talk of love and charity?

I recalled how Agnes Hancock had spoken a word of knowledge to me well before anyone, least of all my barrister, could have foreseen that the police would suddenly and inexplicably change their mind about an obscure terrorist who had already signed his name to a confession. As far as I was concerned, there was power—like the power of dynamite. The only problem was, at the time, I had no matches. That would come later.

Not long afterwards, I met more men who had given their lives to Christ. Chaps such as Peter and Tonto, who had been murderers; Liam, a bomber; Paul, a fellow terrorist; and many more who had come to know Christ and as a result had had their lives turned around for the better. It amazed me to see that God was working in so many other lives, Loyalist as well as Republican.

Sensing the Lord's presence in my cell one day, I fell on my knees and said, 'What do you want me to do while I'm in prison, Lord?'

A thought came to me after I had prayed: 'Billy, I want you to use this time to study, to educate yourself, and to prepare yourself for full-time Christian service after your release from prison.' I could hardly believe my ears: I who had been a terrorist was going to become involved in humanitarian work? Despite my initial scepticism, I shrugged and said, 'At least it's a clear answer to my question.'

The next day I began to act upon God's command. Through my mate Paul I'd heard of a place called the London Bible College. I wrote to the college and requested details about their Bible correspondence course. Soon I was enrolled and studying a book I'd only seen collecting dust in my home all my life. Behind bars I came to see this book as a library containing all the knowledge worth knowing in this and the next life.

I had already learned that life is nothing like the fairytales. If my life story had been one written by Hans Andersen, it would have been at this point that all the clouds would have silver linings. All problems would have faded. I would have no more trials to overcome, and in the fullness of time I would have been quickly released from prison only to become the leading light in Ulster's church scene. It wasn't to be quite so easy as that.

The fact is, my commitment to Christ made life in the H-block difficult. Not only for me but for others, including my wife. God was teaching me that although he paid the price for our salvation on the cross, there is a price to pay for being a Christian. As it says in the Gospel of Luke: 'If anyone would come after me, he must deny himself and take up his cross daily and follow me. For whoever wants to save his life will lose it, but whoever loses his life for me will save it' (Luke 9:23–24).

Since this is by far the hardest lesson for any new Christian to learn, the best place for me to learn it was in a place like the Maze Prison where I would be faced with fewer distractions and temptations to go wrong.

Anyone who has lived through the early 1980s will recognise the name of the Maze Prison. It was here that Republican and Loyalist prisoners were rounded up together, creating intense friction just as dangerous as any outside the prison.

It was here in 1981 that Republican leader, Bobby Sands, starved himself to death and sparked off a spate of similar protests by Republicans calling themselves 'the Blanket Men'.

With so many Loyalists and Republicans under the same roof, it's no wonder tensions mounted and whole sectors of the prison were unofficial 'no-go' areas. Despite the strict presence of the guards, a sub-culture existed among us prisoners; a sub-culture marked off by boundaries and enforced by the same set of rules which existed out in the streets of Ulster where terror was a normal way of life, not an aberration.

We Loyalists were a decided minority in the Maze which made me very wary of dark corridors or isolated reading rooms. On one occasion I turned up for work, but when I noticed no other Loyalists were there that morning, I ran out of the door and point-blankly refused to go back into the workshop.

The guard shoved me, commanding, 'What's wrong with you? Go back inside.'

'No way,' I retorted. I had an eerie premonition that something bad would happen to me if I stayed in the workshop which was filled with Republicans. I literally dug my heels in and pressed back from the entrance way.

'You're asking for trouble,' the guard warned.

'It'll be solitary confinement for you, and a permanent black mark on your record!'

I shrugged and said, 'I'll wait for a few of my mates to turn up and then maybe I'll go in.'

'It's like that, is it?' he said in a menacing tone of voice. Moments later, the guard twisted my arm behind my back and I was bundled off for disciplinary action. For my insubordination, I was put in a place called 'the boards'—solitary confinement.

As it happened, that particular day a riot did erupt in the workshop. It happened at lunchtime. A number of Loyalists were hospitalised, some with serious injuries and severely broken bones. On the whole, I fared better in my punishment cell than I would have done had I walked into that room that day.

Not long after this, a mate of mine, Kenny, had been warned by the Republicans to get out of 'their' workshop. Now Kenny was a lifer, but he was also a Christian. All of us knew of his life both before and after his conversion. In anyone's eyes he certainly had street credibility. Yet somehow he had managed to put his former life behind him in order to become what I could only describe as a new man. We knew he feared no one, prisoner or guard, but unlike before, when he would step on anyone who got in his way, he now treated everyone with love and respect, regardless of their being Republican or Loyalist. He even respected the guards without sucking up to them.

Kenny took the Republican threats seriously, but he said he had no quarrel with anyone. As the threats persisted, he must have sensed that the Republicans interpreted his passiveness as cowardice. One day, a messenger came up to him in the canteen. 'Kenny boy, this is your last warning. The word is you're dog meat if you go back to work this afternoon. Don't say you haven't been warned.' All eyes were on the pair.

'Go back and tell your friends that I'll take on any one of them with my fists; one to one, like, to settle this matter. If anyone can knock me out, you win—I'll stay out of your way. But if I knock your man out, you lot can get off my back and I go where I please. Is it a deal?' The word got back to the Republicans, but Kenny had no takers from the ones who had made the threat.

Days passed and Kenny continued to turn up for work in the same shop. Many of us began to worry about Kenny. He was, after all, one of us. So out of consideration for his safety, and the welfare of all the Loyalists, I approached him during a break since we were on the same wing.

'Look, mate,' I said. 'Have you lost your mind?'

'Why, Billy?'

'Don't act stupid, man. The odds of you staying healthy are slim. It'll be any day now we'll be hearing that you've had your skull cracked open. Why don't you refuse to go back to that workshop?'

Smiling, Kenny replied, 'I know what you're saying, Billy. But the way I see it, I don't worry about the threats. Just look at Daniel in the lions' den. He trusted the Lord and he came out in one piece.'

I shook my head and felt cross at his cocksure manner. 'I'll level with you. I personally want to stay alive until I can get out of this place. You're dicing with death, man, and even though you think you're doing the right thing, it's not exactly the way we see things.'

There was no use talking to Kenny, though. He wasn't afraid, and went back to work the next day despite another warning from a Republican spokesman.

During a tea break, Kenny sat down and began to unwrap a packet of biscuits. For some reason, the guard stepped out of the room for a moment. As if on cue, a lone figure lifted an urn of vigorously boiling water from the blue flames of a gas stove. Suddenly the room fell silent. Kenny looked up to see why everything had gone quiet. The same instant, the man threw the steaming water into Kenny's face, scalding his neck, head and shoulders.

Screaming and tumbling to the floor, Kenny kicked the table over in agony, and slithered on his belly towards the door and safety. He reached the doors in the nick of time. The guard caught hold of his hands and dragged him into the hallway. Had he delayed even a few seconds longer, the mob would have been onto him and beaten him to death with the chairs. The guard called for reinforcements and had Kenny rushed to hospital where he was treated for first and second degree burns to his head, face, neck, shoulders and upper body. His skin had been badly scalded.

Over the next twelve months, Kenny went through a series of skin grafts and other burns-related operations.

A year-and-a-half later, Kenny sent a message to the man who had led the attack. In it, he said that he loved him and that he prayed for him every day. Kenny sent this message through the prison chaplain—the only other man in the Maze with courage enough to deliver such a message. The Republicans almost collapsed with disbelief. The reaction was the same among us Loyalists. I had heard sermons telling us to turn the other cheek when someone strikes us, but until then I'd never known anyone who was prepared to do it. In the months ahead, I would meet others like Kenny, both among the Loyalists and the Republicans.

I have already said how the Christian faith calls us to pick up our cross and follow Jesus along our own via dolorosa. Because of his faith, my mate Kenny landed in hot water, literally, for his stand against on-going sectarian hatred in Belfast's prisons. Kenny's sacrifice wasn't wasted, however. His actions proved to everyone in that prison that love is far more powerful than hatred. Kenny had the dynamite *and* the pack of matches. I wondered how long it would be before I would have to withstand so great a test of my fledgling faith.

As it happens, my first trial was to come from a most unexpected quarter, and while it was hardly life-threatening like Kenny's, it was an agonising time for me nonetheless. The problem was Ed, my new cell mate.

Ed had a pornographic magazine which was being circulated from cell to cell. His first words to me when he saw me glance at the cover were, 'Help yourself, mate!'

At these words I felt the old surge of lustful joy at the hours of pleasure these provocative and lewd pictures would bring me in the privacy of my fantasies.

I soon picked up the magazine. To my horror, my first glance at the pages of women's naked bodies caused me to flush with embarrassment. I felt the blood rush to my cheeks. What was happening? I used to push this stuff for fun and profit. Then it dawned on me: my mind was now under the control of the Holy Spirit, and he was saying in no uncertain terms to put the magazine down. Like a child who had planned to be naughty, I paused for a long moment, wondering who would win the battle raging in my flesh: God or the devil.

Then I summoned my full will and put the magazine back on Ed's shelf.

For the rest of the day I managed to keep busy enough not to think about Ed's magazine. But I found to my disgust that even as I tried to pray before going to bed, my mind kept straying back to those sexy images only a few inches away from my quivering hands. This was the worst torture I'd ever known. My spirit wanted to be pure and righteous, but my body lusted after the naked women. I'd never fully broken my addiction to pornography, so my struggle was like an alcoholic's and his bottle.

As I lay in bed, I literally began to sweat as a result of the great tension I felt. Not knowing what else to do, I prayed, 'Dear Jesus, I know you were a man, and so you understand my struggle. I don't want to look at that magazine. Please show me what to do.'

Ed must have seen me sweating. 'You all right, man?' he said, looking at me out of the corner of his eye.

'Yeah, I'm OK,' I lied. Then I decided to be truthful with Ed. 'Actually, I'm not OK, Ed. I have a problem and you can help me. I'm a Christian . . . I haven't been one very long. And, well. . .'

'Yeah?' said Ed in a tentative voice. 'So what's that got to do with me, man?'

'It's your porno book, Ed. It's driving me crazy, but I don't want to look at it. Being a Christian doesn't mean I'm brain dead, if you know what I mean. I wonder if you could get rid of it. It's not really any good anyway. It gets to you after a while.'

I fully expected Ed either to laugh in my face or to tell me to mind my own business. In fact, he did neither. He cocked his head and said, 'I'll think about that, man.' He then rolled over in his bed and said nothing more.

In the morning the magazine was gone. I don't know what Ed did with it, and I didn't ask him. The best thing was that the agony I'd felt the night before had gone just as mysteriously.

I stretched out on my bed and smiled. But there were more problems brewing, even as I lay there thinking I'd got this Christianity thing all sussed out.

# Chapter Thirteen

Earlier I said that the Maze Prison was a veritable powder keg as both Loyalist and Republican terrorists were housed under one roof. Incidents such as the one involving Kenny, and worse, were not unusual.

Common sense would suggest that putting bitter enemies together is a sure formula for trouble. Week in and week out new incidents were taking place, but still the authorities insisted on keeping the status quo firmly in place.

Despite the brutal attack on my mate Kenny, Republicans weren't the only perpetrators of the trouble. I remember one time when Simon, a Loyalist, laid in wait in the canteen for a chance to attack a hapless Republican. Most of us Loyalists knew Simon was up to something, but we just turned a blind eye to it. We thought he was a bit mad, really.

Before long his big chance came. One of the leading Republicans came into the canteen at lunch at the same time Simon was in there. Without anyone noticing him, Simon slipped into the kitchen and picked up an urn of boiling water. His plan was to repay the Republicans for what they had done to Kenny—even though Kenny had forgiven his attackers.

Without so much as a word of warning, Simon flung the scalding water over the other man. Of course the man was taken into hospital and I never did hear how he fared after that. Reprisals led to reprisals which led to still more reprisals. Daily, men were being treated for scalds, cuts or broken bones in the prison surgery.

Such was the climate in the Maze Prison: we were all caught up in a vicious cycle of hate and there was no way out. The problems of sectarian conflict continued to escalate until finally the Loyalists began to protest for segregration. Even I had to admit that it seemed the only way forward.

For the most part, official protests were noted by the prison authorities, but by and large all such political grievances were ignored.

Not surprisingly, before long, the powers that be in the Loyalist camp decided that the time had come for us to call the nation's attention to the internal conflicts stemming from mixing Republicans with Loyalists in the Maze Prison. The word was put out among all Loyalists that there was to be a big bust up on a particular afternoon. All of us were expected to take part in the demonstration.

At the agreed time, the protest began. A handful of leaders shouted orders, and men obeyed. The sheer numbers of prisoners in relation to the guards meant that the guards were effortlessly bundled off the wing. Scores of men surged and swarmed like a wild sea. Tables in the recreation room were turned over and used to blockade the doors; windows were smashed; washrooms were destroyed.

At one point, I was ordered to start smashing up whatever I could lay my hands on, as part of the morning's disruption.

Ted, one of the prisoners whom I knew to be a Christian, happened to be on the scene. He urged men to return to their cells and stay there. 'Above all,' he shouted, 'don't do anything you'll regret later.'

'Ted's right,' called my mate, Bobby. 'Let's get back to our cell.'

The two of us ran for our cell, locking ourselves well out of harm's way once we got inside.

There was no question in my mind; I wasn't about to smash up anything. Even as we could hear furniture and fixtures being smashed to the right and left of our cell, ours was a haven of peace in a sea of chaos.

Men rushing by would stop and shout inside for us to start smashing up our cell. Sam, one of the leaders of the paramilitaries whom I knew from before my imprisonment, rushed by and skidded to a halt. Peering incredulously inside, he sputtered, 'What do you two old women think you're doing just standing there? Get busy tearing that place apart! That's an order, McFetridge!'

Bobby grabbed my arm, saying, 'Don't listen to him, Billy! Stand your ground.'

'I'm telling you, McFetridge: you start smashing up that cell or we'll get in and do it for you,' Sam said. I could see he meant business. 'Now move it!'

I turned to Bobby and whispered in a hoarse voice, 'I'd better do something to keep in good with them. If I lose face I'll never live it down.' Reluctantly, I lifted a chair and, grunting, I bashed the window with three smart blows. 'What the . . . ?' I said aloud. Try as I might to knock the window out, it wouldn't break. Even with my mightiest swing, the chair merely bounced harmlessly off the pane.

'See, Billy,' said Bobby. 'It doesn't want to break. You've had a go, now stop this madness!'

I felt like a man possessed. I was determined to break that window. I gave the glass four more reverberating knocks. With each mighty swing of the chair, I expected the shards of shattered glass to shower down upon us, but with each blow the heavy wooden chair bounced harmlessly off.

In frustration, I poked the leg of the chair at a smaller pane of glass at the top of the window which tinkled to the ground outside.

Bobby frowned and said, 'I understand why you think you had to do that, Billy, but now it means that the screws will split us up.' I knew he was right; even though the pane of glass I broke was small, I would be charged along with all the other rioters when the guards spotted the damage. Before long, I'd be put in a different cell and that would be that.

The pandemonium in the wing eventually quietened down, and the prison authorities regained control of the situation. Though the demonstration was short, the desired outcome was achieved. Soon a so-called 'defacto' segregation was introduced and is still in effect today. By and large, I believe that's why today we hear of less friction in the Maze Prison as compared to in the early 1980s.

As Bobby had said, we two were separated. I confessed to having broken the window pane during the protest so Bobby wouldn't be punished. I was charged under prison rules with destroying Government property and disobeying the direct order of the Governor to move to designated accommodation.

For this infraction, I lost privileges such as association, one visit per month, use of tuck shop and use of education facilities. This was tough, but the hardest thing was being separated from Bobby who could have taught me so much more about this recent commitment I'd made to Christ. Why did I feel as if I needed to participate in the destruction when Bobby never lifted a finger? I could see that I had much to learn about the gospel of peace.

For the first couple of days I was very angry at myself for allowing myself to be intimidated by Sam. *And you call yourself a Christian*, I repeated over and over in my mind. *Your conversion was nothing more than a ploy to curry favour with the authorities!* For the first time in months, I was feeling condemned.

One morning, while I was sitting feeling sorry for myself, it dawned on me that it was Satan who condemned me, not Christ. In fact, Christ was there with me, suffering my punishment, standing by me closer than even my mate Bobby, despite my rash actions. This realisation made the whole affair almost worthwhile. I was wrong to think that I needed Bobby, or any other human being, for as Paul wrote to Timothy: 'Train yourself to be godly. For physical training is of some value, but godliness has value for all things, holding promise for both the present life and the life to come' (1 Timothy 4:7–8).

The words stood out like a neon sign: *train yourself*. I didn't need another person to train me; Christians must allow the Holy Spirit to instruct them through God's word, the Bible. Moreover, Paul told Timothy to *practise* godliness. This is not an option, it's a command.

'Oh Lord,' I whispered, 'forgive me for thinking

you are disgusted with me. Hear my prayer, Lord, I'm lost. Guide me in the way you want me to go. Forgive me for my lack of faith. Amen.' As I prayed, it felt as if a sixteen-stone man had climbed off my back. My problems certainly hadn't gone away, but I felt strong in the Lord.

Putting away all thoughts of self-condemnation, I turned in my Bible and read Psalm 40 which begins: 'I waited patiently for the Lord; he turned to me and heard my cry. He lifted me out of the slimy pit, out of the mud and mire; he set my feet on a rock and gave me a firm place to stand' (verses 1–2).

From that day on, I became a willing pupil, putting all my faith in Jesus.

Over the next four years, I dutifully studied the word of God through the correspondence course from the London Bible College, and in my own quiet times. I was amazed at the amount of wisdom which is contained in passage after passage of the Bible; wisdom which was useful not only for the enrichment of my soul, but also for the enrichment of my long days behind bars. For the first time in my life, I was entering into substantial relationships with other people who were fast becoming friends. Because I had learned from the Bible to 'esteem others as better than yourself', I was able to make friends in ways I hadn't known were possible. I found joy in giving without expecting to receive anything in return. I even began to muster a rudimentary love for my IRA enemies. At last, I could understand something of what made my mate Kenny tick.

Even Christine, the one person who knew me best, and who had seen me at my worst, could tell that I was a new man. We had some of the most tender moments of our lives in those short prison visits. I wasn't falling in love with Christine, I was growing in love with her. I wanted her to know that the source of this new growth was God.

From time to time I felt as if she feared the new me. Not because I was unpleasant to be around; on the contrary, she felt uncomfortable around me because I had become a virtual stranger. Once, my wife admitted that she didn't know me any more. I took this as something good. I was a new man. This new man could be the father and husband the old man could never be.

I longed for the day when I would leave prison and make up for the years of pain I inflicted on both my wife and Christopher. Meanwhile, I was determined to be a loving and kind husband and father—despite the bars which separated me from my family and home.

You can imagine, then, how awful I felt when I heard through the grapevine that Christine had begun to see another man. I refused to believe the rumours until one Saturday morning when she came to visit me. I could tell by her face even before she spoke that something was wrong. I dreaded what she might have to say, but sat quietly as Christine admitted to having an affair. But she hadn't come to ask for my forgiveness; she had come to ask for a divorce.

I prayed silently as I listened to her spell out her reasons for wanting to leave me. Every one of her charges was true: I'd been unfaithful; I'd been a criminal; I wasn't a good father. In my heart I couldn't deny one charge. But a new joy surged up in my heart because I knew that the Billy she knew was gone for ever; dead to his bondage to Satan.

'Christine,' I said eagerly, 'I can't deny what you've said. But surely you'll believe me when I tell you that I'm a new man—you've said as much yourself. In a mere two years I come up for parole, and no doubt will be out on licence. We could begin anew.' I tried to squeeze my whole body through the barrier between us to hold her in my arms.

'I'm sorry, Billy,' Christine said. 'I'll admit you do seem like a new man, but I just don't trust you any more. What if you go back to the way you were?'

I felt all the blood rush out of my face as she said this. *No, God, don't let this be the way it's to end*, I screamed inwardly.

She spoke again. 'I'd like to stay friends with you, but I insist that we have a divorce. Any trust we might have had is now dead. That's my final word.'

That night I went down on my knees, praying that this trial would pass me by. I can still recall the simple prayer I spoke at the time: 'Dear Jesus, I'm not the same man Christine knew. I'm a Christian now. I don't want a divorce. Thank you, Lord. Amen.'

For a few hours I felt remarkably calm, almost placid, as I read, paced the floor of my cell or lay on my bed. But suddenly I felt a stirring in my body. On the shelf was a photo of Christine and Christopher. I grabbed it and looked into their smiling faces. 'I belong in this picture!' I roared at the top of my lungs. 'Do you hear? I belong there! Not some other bloke!'

Before I knew what I was doing, I had flung the picture against the wall, smashing the wooden frame and glass cover. The noise of the tinkling glass set me off swearing in a way I'd never heard myself swear ever before—even as a trigger man with the

UDA. I swore until I couldn't even form proper curses, just gutteral grunts and primitive-sounding words.

'I've got to get out of here!' I roared. I began to pace back and forth like a lion in a circus cage. My pacing increased until I was running back and forth in my cell—now slamming into the wall, now stumbling. 'Let me out of here! I've got to get to my wife and son!' I yelled.

'Shut up!' called someone from the hall. Writhing with anger, I clutched a wooden chair by its back and swung it with all my might into the window of the cell. To my surprise, whereas the last time I'd pulled a stunt like this the chair had bounced harmlessly off the pane, this time the window shattered into hundreds of tiny fragments, showering glass and bits of wood all over the floor.

By now I was insane with rage, and the next thing I knew I had torn the bed apart. With one blow of my fist, I sent my bookshelf crashing to the floor.

'McFetridge, what the devil do you think you're playing at in there?' I turned and saw another inmate peering into my cell. I charged at him and pressing my face to within an inch of his, I let fly another string of four letter words and curses which only made me crazier still.

Seconds later, the door to the cell burst open and I was tumbled to the floor by three other men and dragged down the hall.

Constrained now by three guards, I sat shaking in a chair and moaning like a wounded bear.

To my relief, instead of bullying me, the guards were trying to calm me down. 'Take it easy, mate,' said one. 'You're under too much pressure; anybody can see that. Nobody's cross with you for busting up your cell like that.'

'Look, here comes the doctor now,' said the other.

'He'll patch you up in no time,' said the third, patting me on the shoulder. 'You just relax now, lad.'

The doctor walked into the room and immediately handed me a cup. 'Here, drink this,' he said.

'What is it?' I asked. I felt a sharp pain as I lifted my hand to take the cup. In my rage I had grazed my knuckles and bruised my head and arms.

'You just drink it. You'll feel streets better for it.'

I obeyed silently. In a few minutes it was just as the doctor had said. I felt as if I had stepped outside of my body, leaving my emotional upset and all my problems inside it. The drink was a powerful tranquilliser called largactil. It's an anti-psychotic drug which sedates the central nervous system. The doctor gave me a triple dose.

After waiting a few more minutes, the doctor got on with his treatment of my cuts. Despite my shredded skin and the deep abrasions, I was feeling no pain. When he was finished, I felt blissfully unconcerned about my problems—even the thought of Christine sleeping with another man didn't faze me.

As I sat there with a stupid grin on my face, Jim Hughes, the prison chaplain, suddenly came into view. At least I think it was one chaplain. I could see three of him.

'Sir,' I said, 'why are there three of you?'

Chaplain Hughes patted me on the shoulder and said, 'It's the largactil I reckon, Billy. Now then, what's all the fuss about tonight? That's quite a mess you made of your cell, lad.'

My mind reeled to grasp what he was talking about. Suddenly a heaviness filled my heart at what I had done. The heaviness was due more to the foulness of my language than to my violence. I choked out my words, 'Sir, my language. Where did it come from? I'm a Christian. . .'

He cut me off by putting up his hand like a traffic cop. 'There, there, Billy. You're under more stress than's healthy for a man.'

I shook my head in shame and lapsed into a silent stupor until my head got heavier and heavier and I fell asleep.

After that incident, I was able to carry on a normal life, working hard by day and studying my Bible by night. I had many opportunities to spend time with other men who had become Christians in the Maze. Here was the only place in Ulster where ex-IRA and ex-UDA men could experience communion together as brothers in Christ.

It was when I realised that I could love my former enemies, and that they could love me in Christ, that I felt that indeed I'd received a full pardon. Better still, I was able to grant full pardon to others. The prison bars were in fact immaterial to this experience, except that it took losing my civil freedom to find true freedom.

Through my involvement with the Christian community in the Maze, I had met James McIlroy, the Director of Prison Fellowship Northern Ireland which has its headquarters at 39 University Street, Belfast. In getting to know him, I let it be known that I felt God was preparing me for full-time Christian work. I wondered if he would take my words seriously. To my delight, he was as excited about the future as I was. He even indicated that he would be pleased if when I was freed, I'd come and see him for a job as a field-worker for Prison Fellowship. Since I wanted him to know all there was to know about me, I confided in him that my marriage was dissolving. I didn't spare him any of the details of my sordid past life, but I assured him that I was a changed man.

'Billy, believe me,' he had said, 'I can see you love the Lord.' His words came as a great comfort to me for I was beginning to wonder if I was merely kidding myself. It was at this point that I asked James if he could go and visit Christine to see if my marriage could be saved. James saw Christine on a number of occasions, but her mind was made up—our marriage was definitely over.

By the summer of 1986, I had served five years of my sentence and thereby had earned a parole—the first of three I would have before my release in 1987.

As soon as I was on the street, I went to see Christine at her house. As it happens her other man was visiting when I turned up. The old Billy would have made an ugly scene, possibly even threatened to kill the man who would steal his wife. The new Billy kept a civil tongue in his head. Oh, I let this bloke know that I didn't think much of him, then I told Christine I wanted her back. But when I had finished, I simply got up and left. No chairs had been broken; no threats had been made.

A few days later, I managed to get Christine to agree to meet me on her own. I felt sure that if we could talk this out in a neutral place, she'd see my love for her had actually grown in the five years of my imprisonment. Since I had always had a good relationship with Christine's mum, I phoned her and told her my problem. To her credit, Christine's mother kindly agreed to allow us to use her flat for the entire evening.

As I recall it, the meeting was cordial, and I felt confident that God would make this untoward situation right; after all, he had done so much already in my life. I was sure he wanted my wife and I to remain together.

However, as the evening wore on, it became abundantly apparent that Christine was resolute in her determination to finish with me. 'But Christine,' I argued, 'I'll be free in a couple of years. You'll see, I'll make it up to you.'

'No, Billy. It's over now. I want a divorce and that's all there is to it.' I could see she was determined to make a clean break of it. Why she decided to do it now after five years, I don't know.

While on parole I had heard about the Elim Church in Larne and decided to go to the Sunday morning service. There I met a man called Liam and his wife Maric. He was a Dublin-based singer who had become a Christian some years ago.

As we chatted, I told him about my past and how I became a Christian in prison.

'Billy, that's an amazing story. Have you ever told it to a church group?'

'No, why?'

'Would you like to come down to Dublin to take part in an outreach to the city?'

My immediate reply was, 'No.' For one thing, I needed special permission to travel into the Republic from Ulster; secondly, I was too nervous to stand up before a crowd of strangers and bare my soul, as it were.

'I'm sorry to hear that, Billy,' was his terse reply. I

could see he was disappointed. 'But we'll be praying for you anyway.'

During my second parole in 1986, I wrote to Liam and Marie to keep them informed of my news. He wrote back, and as he had the last time I saw him, Liam spoke about my giving my testimony again. 'Billy, you really should tell others about what God's been doing in your life,' he wrote. 'It'll give glory to God!'

Since he put it like that, I didn't feel as reluctant to tell others what had happened in my life. When I wrote back, I said so, adding, 'But I'm sure I'll not be able to get permission to travel to Dublin to speak. I promise, though, that at least I'll look into it.' With that, I posted the letter with my heart feeling strangely warmed by this jolly couple from Southern Ireland.

The next day I went to the prison governor and made an enquiry about my travelling down to Dublin. To my amazement, the prison officials had no qualms about letting a former terrorist travel freely into the South of Ireland. To make a long story short, I ended up contacting my new friends Liam and Marie, and I agreed to give my testimony in Dublin.

Giving my testimony was a lot easier than I'd expected it to be. In fact it was over before I knew what I had done. The most remarkable incident was that after I had told the story of my life, a young Swiss woman came over to speak to me. I noticed her standing to my left as I chatted with someone else. She was tall, with brushed back dark chestnut hair, and she had soft brown eyes. I liked her casual style of dress: a red woollen jumper, blue jeans and tennis shoes. When the other person walked off, she stepped up to me. 'My name is Martha Grunenwald,' she said, meeting my eye and giving me a firm handshake. 'I'm a short-term missionary vorking here in Dublin. I come from Svitzerland.'

'Glad to meet you,' I stammered.

'It vas an amazing coincidence to hear you speak tonight,' she said in her strange Swiss–Dublin accent.

'Why's that?' I asked.

'I yust finished reading Rita Nightingale's book, *Freed for Life*, and I'm very impressed by her story. Have you read it?'

'Yes,' I said. 'Why did you like it?' I asked.

As she talked about Rita's courage and faith, I couldn't help but notice how friendly this outgoing Swiss woman was. In fact everyone that night treated me as if I was a long-lost brother instead of a former member of the UDA.

I carried on talking to born-again Roman Catholics and Southern Irish Protestants over tea, but all too soon I had to say goodbye for I was due back in at the Maze.

On the return journey to Belfast, it dawned on me that I had spent the evening among the very people I once hated and feared, only now I could honestly say that I felt genuine love and concern for them. I couldn't wait to tell James McIlroy about the amazing things which had happened that evening in Dublin. Stranger things were brewing that evening: for I had no way of knowing then that soon after, this outgoing Swiss missionary would become a steady penfriend, and indeed that by 1989 Martha Grunenwald would become my wife.

By 1986 God had shown me a number of times that he was pleased to use even a crooked stick such as myself to draw straight lines. I had on a number of occasions led other men to the Lord, and I had done very well on the London Bible College correspondence course. What's more, James McIlroy's invitation to join him in his work in Ulster's prisons was the confirmation I needed to be sure I was on the right track.

The one real dark cloud in my life was my marriage. How could I hope to help others when I couldn't even keep my own family together, I wondered? And anyway, the Bible teaches that divorce is wrong. I knew now not to give in to self-condemnation as that is a trick of Satan. Indeed, the Bible teaches that Satan is our arch foe who stands before God accusing us of every manner of sin, but God doesn't hear Satan, and when we repent, he is only too happy to forgive and cover our shortcomings with love (see Revelation 12:10). Knowing this was helpful, for at least I didn't work myself up into a fury, even though I still grieved over what had become of the love between Christine and me.

One night, while laying on my bed and praying that my marriage would be preserved, I heard the Lord say clearly that I was to let go of Christine and to trust only him. 'Are you sure, Lord?' I asked. There was no reply, but I knew I'd heard right the first time.

'OK, then, I release Christine and trust only you, Lord. Amen.' I won't say that this was an easy thing to do, but I was resolved to obey. To my amazement, my anxiety ceased and I was able to find joy once more.

Not long afterwards, James McIlroy invited me to come and visit him at the Prison Fellowship drop-in centre and this I did gladly. I spent many happy hours in the centre getting to know James and some of the other people who made up the Prison Fellowship team.

Walking around the refurbished Georgian town house, I envisioned myself working alongside people to whom I could relate—men and women who felt rejected by their families, ex-terrorists, people wrongly accused of crimes, men who had lost their wives while they were behind bars. I began to see every event which happened in my life as part of a greater scheme; as part of what Christian writer Dr Francis Schaeffer once called the 'warp and the woof of life' with God as the master weaver. Moreover, it made Romans 8:28 a reality in my misbegotten life: 'In all things God works for the good of those who love him, who have been called according to his purpose.'

I certainly never rejoiced in all the bad things which had happened in my life, but I did rejoice in the fact that I could draw upon my own experiences to help others find a way forward in practical and spiritual ways. All that remained was for my final months of prison to expire, and then I could get on with my life as a servant of God.

# Chapter Fourteen

My prison sentence finished on 24th April 1987, and since I no longer had a wife and home to go to, I asked my mother if I could move back in with her. Characteristically, she said, 'Of course.' So for the second time during my adult life, my mother was there to support me. Only now my relationship with her was radically transformed. There would be no secrets between the two of us, no late night comings and goings, and for sure there would be no more betrayal of her love by my crimes and gun running.

As soon as I could, I went to see James to find out how things stood with his offer for me to work with him. After chatting to him and thinking through my options, he suggested something that took me by complete surprise. 'Billy, I think you ought to consider applying to Belfast Bible College to round off the foundation work which you began through your prison correspondence course.'

I replied cautiously, 'When I came down here today, I wasn't expecting anyone to suggest that I attend a college. After all, I hardly made it through school, and besides I'm thirty-seven years old. Most of the other students there will be only half my age and certainly better educated than I am. I don't think I could handle it.' I sat back in my seat and glared dolefully out of the window.

James smiled. 'I know you have some doubts, but why don't we just apply and see what comes of it?' he said with the cool wisdom born of his years of living by faith. 'They can only say no and that'll settle it.'

'What if they say yes?' I demanded.

'Let's cross that bridge when we come to it, eh?'

I shrugged and agreed. After all, if it was God speaking to me through James about Belfast Bible College, I had no right to balk, for I had given God permission to be my Lord.

In a few weeks, I was called in for an interview. In a blind panic I asked James if he'd come along with me to hold my hand, which he did gladly. It was a long day of meeting people, looking over the college and talking about my life to people whom I didn't know.

At the end of the day, I was called in with James to meet with the selection committee. There I was told that the Belfast Bible College was pleased to accept me as a student. A chill ran up the length of my spine and I felt lightheaded. I honestly hadn't expected this.

On the way home I told James that I would accept the place at the college. 'I just pray I don't fail all my courses.' I looked over at him for reassurance. James only smiled and patted me on the knee. I'd have given anything to know what he was thinking about my prospects as a student.

Until then I had never lived by faith. I had always either been on the dole or had a job of some sort.

But in September of 1987, without any visible means of support, I embarked on my career as a full-time student. I want to emphasise that I went back into the classroom with fear and loathing. The proverbial carrot which goaded me on was the hope of serving God, possibly with the Prison Fellowship Northern Ireland. This and this alone helped me to find courage to push on towards the other end of the long, dark tunnel.

Another factor which encouraged me was the friendly letters I was receiving from time to time from one Martha Grunenwald. To be honest, I was flattered that she desired to keep up with our friendship even though she lived in Dublin and I in Belfast. But I was always very frank in my return letters, pointing out that I was a married man until my divorce was final, and that I had a prison record. Privately, I expected that such blunt facts would put her off writing to me. Yet I would be a liar if I said that I didn't want to correspond with such a stimulating young woman.

I was impressed by her candid nature and her freshness; moreover, I was impressed by her faith in Christ which had prompted her to give up a comfortable home and a successful job in Switzerland as a nurse, in order to respond to an inner prompting to come to Ireland to get involved with a low-budget Christian ministry looking after the needs of Dublin's street people.

At this point I want to mention a very significant event which took place during the summer of 1988 during the college break. What happened was every bit as important to me as my conversion to Christ in prison.

At the time I was working as a Teen Challenge

staff worker in South Wales. This particular incident took place in an old barn during a mission led by Pastor John Macey, the Director of Teen Challenge, UK.

Throughout the whole service I felt as if God was standing before me. This sensation led to a powerful conviction of my own sinfulness. It's not that I felt God was saying I was unworthy; rather, it was me saying it about myself in comparison to the holy presence I felt so near to me.

It came to me towards the end of the meeting that God was about to do a special thing in my life. What that thing was to be, I didn't know.

Pastor Macey made a special appeal to the congregation, saying, 'Anyone who wants the baptism of the Holy Spirit may come to the front and we'll lay-on hands and pray for you.'

I had heard this curious term many times before at different churches, so I knew what to expect. What's more, I had gone forward in other meetings for the laying-on of hands, but nothing had ever happened. I had no doubt that the gifts described in the New Testament were for today, but for some inexplicable reason I seemed unable to break through the barrier which was fixed between me and the baptism of the Holy Spirit.

Don't misconstrue: certainly when I became a Christian I received the Holy Spirit. I also knew that from time to time our life in the Holy Spirit needs to be *rekindled*, as Paul wrote to Timothy in 2 Timothy 1:6–7. And now, here was an invitation to have more of him. Before a second call was made, I made my way forward with several dozen others and waited for a minister to come to me.

A young man approached me and asked, 'What's your name?'

'Billy,' I replied meekly.

'Lift your hands and praise God.'

Hesitantly, I complied with his instructions.

'You are very special in God's eyes, Billy.' Saying that, he reached out and lightly touched my chest with the palm of his right hand.

No sooner had he touched me than I felt a surge of energy break forth from his hand, hitting my solar plexus. The impact was painless, but lifted me off the ground and knocked me back a few feet onto the floor. Again, I felt no pain, not even when I crashed into the rough wood of the barn floor.

As I lay there, dazed and confused, I was over-come with a profound sense of guilt for past, unconfessed sins which reduced me to tears. This lasted for a few minutes. When my tears stopped, I began to mutter. I couldn't make out what I was saying, but I was certainly talking nineteen to the dozen by this time.

Gradually I became aware of others around me praying in a language unknown to me. I had heard this sound before and I asked myself, *Could I be speaking in tongues?*

After another ten minutes of chattering away in this new language, I was helped to my feet. I knew that the man who now stood before the Lord was different from the one who had walked into that meeting an hour earlier. I seemed to be freer, happier, more bold in my desire to worship the Lord. If this is the change the baptism of the Holy Spirit brings about in Christians, the change is most definitely for the better. It was impossible to keep my hands down. I wanted to raise them and praise God for all I was worth.

After the meeting broke up an impromptu praise

session erupted again. After half an hour or so of singing and praising God, I finally returned to the Teen Challenge Centre feeling as light as air itself.

The next morning, as I lay in bed, I thought about the events of the night before. Was it all just an emotional flash in the pan? Or was it a genuine, life-changing gift? Maybe it was just a response to the pressure to be seen as 'spiritual'. I decided to see if I could pray in tongues right there off my own bat. There was no preacher, no people, no singing, no pressure to perform. I wouldn't even bother to get on my knees. I'd just lay there in bed and try it. If I couldn't, then I'd know I'd been misled. To my great surprise, I found I could exercise the gift at will.

I began to recognise certain syllables and whole words as I prayed on. It certainly was like a foreign language, maybe Aramaic or Greek. The most interesting thing is that it doesn't come on you like a fit. It's just like a second language you choose to speak when you please. Only you never had to study it!

After a few minutes of muttering and clicking my tongue in this heavenly language, I felt elated and full of praise. I seized my Bible, and as I read I felt as if whole passages I'd seen a dozen times before were alive and full of meaning just for me. After my quiet time, I was definitely sustained for the day ahead of me.

I'm sure the baptism of the Holy Spirit helped me to go back to college and tackle my second year in far better form than the one previous. Of course, I still found study hard, but my mind was now focused squarely on the living God who had demonstrated to me once again that 'our times are in his hands', and, 'Lo, I am with you until the end.' These are two pieces of Scripture I had only known in my mind. After this 'topping-up' with his Spirit, I understood them from first-hand experience.

Another blessing of the baptism of the Holy Spirit was that I found the strength to face the fact of my divorce which had become final around that time. Christine was awarded Christopher, our son, and I would have weekend visitation rights.

I found a letter from Martha waiting for me upon my return to Belfast. Instead of writing back (I'm a terrible letter writer), I arranged for us to meet again through my Dublin friends Liam and Marie.

Martha took the train up to Larne to meet my mother and Christopher. My motives, I know, were transparent: I had marriage on my mind and, much to my delight, Martha didn't seem to object.

Needless to say, though, Martha had some very serious questions to work through before she would ever consent to marry me—not the least was the fact that I was a divorcee, something which posed an even greater problem to her strict Brethren background than the fact that I'd been in prison. Maybe it is better to say that it was her parents' strict Brethren doctrine which was the stumbling block, for Martha's years as a student and travelling in Africa, Europe and Ireland had broadened her outlook considerably. Martha had already written to tell her mother and father about me, and so frequent were the references to me, that I'm sure her parents knew even before Martha that I would pop the question sooner or later. There was no doubt that the Grunenwalds' greatest fears for their adventurous daughter were materialising in the form of this stranger who was not only an ex-terrorist, but a married man as well.

Martha wished to honour her parents whom she loved dearly. I fully understood this, as my love for my own dear mother was equally important to me. In my case, Mum took to Martha immediately, so the ball was squarely in the Grunenwalds' court. Sooner or later, Martha and I would need to obtain her parents' blessing to get married. For the time being, we could do nothing about this.

Another problem with which Martha needed to come to terms was the fact that she had come to Ireland to serve God, not to find a husband. Would marriage put paid to her successful missionary career?

'If you marry me,' I pointed out, 'I hope that you'll work with me among prisoners, Martha. It'll be a new mission field.'

'I had already thought of that, Billy, and I'm glad you said it. I do vant so to carry on telling people about Jesus, even if I became a wife.'

At the end of the weekend visit, Martha said that she wanted to talk to me privately, so we went out for a walk. Without preliminaries she said, 'Billy, I've got total peace about us. I vould like to marry you, but I need time to think things over.'

'Sure, darling,' I said, patting her arm. 'I don't want to rush into anything either. I'm so happy, a few more months won't matter to me now!' To my amazement, I felt a tear come to my eye—a tear of pure joy. I brushed it aside and grinned stupidly at the woman who was to become my life's partner. Then we kissed. It seemed amazing to me that such happiness should come to me when I was nearly forty years old, despite the bad start I'd had in life. *Ours is truly a God of new beginnings*, I thought, as I embraced Martha's slim waist with my eager arms.

After Martha returned to Dublin, I went back to college feeling ready for anything. There's nothing like romance to make a man feel as though he could climb the Matterhorn!

It was then a bomb dropped in the form of a letter which arrived on the desk of the college principal. It had been sent by Martha's missionary headquarters in Dublin at the request of Martha's father. Mr Grunenwald wanted the principal to write to Switzerland to tell him if he felt that I was a suitable match for his daughter.

The principal called in my tutors and after talking over with them my plans to marry Martha, a copy of the letter was sent to me. Unbeknown to me, a small rift was caused in college by my asking Martha to marry me. Whereas some of the tutors were squarely on my side, the principal and some others had reservations about the whole affair owing to the fact of my divorce.

The principal was on the horns of a dilemma: on one side, he couldn't tell Martha's father that he approved 100% of me as a suitable husband for his daughter since I was a divorcee; on the other side, he didn't want to condemn me, for he himself approved of me as a student in the college, and could see that I would be a good prison worker.

In an attempt at wriggling free of the horns, the principal sent me a second letter. In it, he gave me an ultimatum: either I put off marrying Martha until I finished my course of study at the college, or I marry her, but leave immediately without finishing my studies.

I could see that the poor man was in a sticky situation, but I felt that neither he nor anyone else at the college had the right to interfere in our affairs.

In a letter to him I thanked him for his concern, but I made it plain to him that ours was strictly a private affair. Furthermore, I indicated that if Martha consented, then we would become formally engaged and marry at a suitable time.

As the weeks passed and no further mention of my plans to get married surfaced at college, the whole matter was dropped. Meanwhile, Martha's parents came across to Ireland to meet me and it was agreed that we would be married.

My second year of study was anything but easy for me. While I did well enough in a few of my courses, I made a pig's ear of my Greek. By tacit agreement between myself and my Greek tutor, I received a failure grade without having to bother with the final paper.

It wasn't only Greek that foxed me; I found the study of the Old Testament to be a nightmare—I couldn't keep the accounts of prophets, histories, poetry and kings straight. I was so discouraged because these experiences were big blows to my self-esteem.

As so much of my coursework seemed to leave me in a state of confusion, I began to feel as if my initial fears were correct. Bible college was a big mistake. Many's the time I screwed up the courage to meet with the principal to arrange to drop out of college, only to chicken out in the end, walking back to the common room with my books in hand and my tail drooping between my legs like a whipped puppy.

Again and again, the thing which kept me plugging on was the possible job with Prison Fellowship which was waiting for me at the end of the two-year course. So you might be able to understand the sharp pang of dismay I felt the day James McIlroy told me he had decided to resign from Prison Fellowship.

'Of course this means I can't promise you you'll find a job at the drop-in centre,' he said in grave tones. I tried to disguise my hurt as best I could, but I'm sure he knew how I felt. After all, he had devoted so many years of his life to working with ex-prisoners, and he of all men in Belfast would know how insecure and hurt by life men such as myself could be by even the smallest set-backs, let alone big ones like this.

I managed to find my voice after a few moments. 'But why are you leaving?'

'I'm getting too old now, Billy. I feel as if God wants a younger man to take over. You understand that?' I nodded and, standing, I walked out of his office wondering what would come next.

Back at college I had an important-looking letter to cheer me up. During the previous term I'd applied to travel to the United States in the spring of 1989 to take part in a six-week programme sponsored by Prison Fellowship International. That's the prison ministry set up by Chuck Colson, the one-time, so-called 'hatchet man' of the Nixon administration, and the founder of Prison Fellowship International.

Colson himself had landed in prison for his part in the Watergate scandal. Shortly before that he had become a Christian through reading CS Lewis' book, *Mere Christianity*. Chuck Colson had written several books of his own, including *Born Again* and *Life Sentence*, both of which I'd read and been greatly helped by.

I tore open the letter and read the contents

quickly. It was indeed good news: I had been accepted on the programme and would not only get to spend a month in America, but I'd be working with Chuck Colson himself. I was over the moon! For me, the chance to travel to the United States was a once-in-a-lifetime opportunity. All my life I had wanted to go there, and now I would be able to see for myself what the place is really like. Better still, it wouldn't be a fortnight at Disneyland or Miami; it would be a month of meeting real Americans in their homes and places of worship. *Thank you, Lord!* I sang in my heart. *USA, here I come!*

The departure date was a month away, so I needed to get moving on making a visa application. Taking all the necessary paperwork to the American consulate, I knew there'd be some questions about my imprisonment. I didn't worry, though, because I felt sure that my present life would speak volumes about my conversion. What's more, when the officials saw that I was going to work with an international prison ministry, then they'd see that it was precisely because of my background that I was asked to join with Chuck Colson.

The man who interviewed me was a classical bureaucrat. He showed not a flicker of emotion as he processed my application. When he saw in my paperwork that I'd been arrested, he asked me to explain the circumstances.

'Well,' I sputtered, 'I was once involved in a bit of trouble in Larne.' He waited for me to say more. I felt the blood rush into my cheeks. 'It wasn't much, really. And anyway, I'm a new man now. You see, I'm going to the States to help others who've gone wrong with the law.'

'I see here that you were charged under the

Prevention of Terrorism Act, Northern Ireland,' he said matter of factly.

I could only nod.

Without saying a word, he took out a card and wrote something on it. He slipped it into a folder and dismissed me. Two days later, I received a letter from the consulate. I was told that due to my status as a former terrorist, the United States Justice Department had deemed me as *persona non grata*. My application for an American visa was denied.

My initial response was shock. Surely, I reasoned, there had been some mistake. The old Billy McFetridge had died, and the one applying to go to America was a new man. As the finality of the letter sank in, my shock gave way to anger. Was I to be punished indefinitely for the mistakes of my youth? How could they do this to me? And where was God in all this? Didn't he want me to go to America?

Later, after I'd had time to cool down and pray about the matter, it occurred to me that I never once asked God if he wanted me to go to America. It had been my own idea right from the start.

I went into my bedroom and dropped down on my knees and prayed, 'Dear Lord, please forgive me for saying you may control my life, when I then go and make my own plans without so much as asking you what you think. Please teach me to be truly submissive to your will. Help me to learn to want to do what you want me to do. Amen.' It was one of the simplest prayers I'd ever sent up. But one of the hardest to mean. Yet I truly *wanted* to mean it. I was learning that a big part of faith is exercising the will, not the emotions.

The curious thing for me was that while I was discouraged about the way things had turned out regarding my prospects of working with Prison Fellowship, Northern Ireland, and now my not going to America to work with prisoners, I wasn't put off the idea of doing Christian work among convicts. I still had the inner strength to face whatever was to come. For even though my job prospects looked bleak and I felt scared, I trusted that God was already one step ahead of me.

I left college in June 1989, and since I had no job I had no choice but to go on the dole. I found work as a volunteer at the Larne YMCA where the youth leader was a former prisoner, Eddie, who had also become a Christian. I told Eddie that I felt sure God wanted me in prison work. 'Well why don't you apply, Billy?' was his common-sense reply. So I did. After all, I had nothing to lose and everything to gain.

I sent the letter to the new director of the Prison Fellowship, Frank Rea, to make a formal application for a job. I said I'd do anything, even sweep the floor. In his return letter, he thanked me for my interest, but pointed out that there was no chance of my finding a permanent paid post at that time. However, he added, 'I'd like you to come and see me and my secretary Patricia, as we are thinking of employing a number of ACE workers.' ACE is a Government scheme to give short-term work to the unemployed. Prison Fellowship, it seemed, could offer employment to two people, one full time and the other part time.

I accepted immediately and rang through to Patricia to arrange an appointment.

After spending the better part of the morning with Frank, he wanted to know over lunch if I'd agree to come to work on the ACE scheme. I didn't have to think twice. I said I would.

'You'll need to make a formal application, Billy,' he warned. 'And you'll need to provide us with three references. Even then, I can't promise you anything.' I said I understood, and as soon as I got home that evening, I began to fill out the form he had given me.

My interview was three weeks later, and soon after that I was told that the full-time post was mine if I wanted it.

I started at the centre as soon as possible, but because I did not have security clearance, I was not allowed in Belfast's prisons. In time I would be given clearance and, as a result, I felt confident that I had indeed found my life's work.

Things were at last looking up. Martha and I were married on 30th September 1989, and we set up our first home in Larne.

One of the biggest struggles I faced in those days as an ACE worker was money. Although the wage of £80 a week was better than being on the dole, such low pay would never do for a married man.

Despite money worries, the work was every bit as satisfying as I'd suspected it might be. Seeing how others conformed their lives to God's will, or how broken lives were healed in miraculous ways, gave me the courage to continue my work knowing that at the end of the twelve-month ACE programme, I might be back on the dole once again.

# Chapter Fifteen

The weeks marched by, turning into months, and since my work with the Prison Fellowship was due to end after the twelve-month period sponsored by the ACE programme, it looked as if I was to become a newly-wed and made redundant all within one year. As it turned out, though, my boss Frank Rea asked me if I would be interested in staying on as a full-time member of staff.

After turning to God in prayer and talking it over with Martha, I told Frank that I'd be only too pleased to take up the offer.

Today, on any given day of the week, I'm busy in the Prison Fellowship drop-in centre in University Street, Belfast. While our main concern is the welfare of the prisoners themselves, a good bit of our work is taken up with looking after the families of the men who are in prison in Ulster. Although Christine is no longer my wife, I've never forgotten the pain she had to endure during the years of my imprisonment. She was on her own with no one to care about her or her needs, nor those of our son,

Christopher other than James, who kept in touch regularly and organised transport so that she was able to visit me on a regular basis. If only she, and others like her, had known about a God who loved them, and an organisation called Prison Fellowship. As it happens she didn't, and even today many don't know we are here to serve them at no cost to them or the State. This is a great tragedy. I take special pride in the fact that entire families may find a warm and clean house in Belfast to come to when they are in the city visiting family members who are behind bars. Even if folk tell us they have no interest in knowing about Christ, they're still most welcome in our centre.

Having said that, the most exciting thing about working for Prison Fellowship Northern Ireland is that while we have the physical and material needs of our clients uppermost in our outreach, we are a Christian organisation serving all of Ulster.

Since this is so, our hope is to bring the gospel to men and women in prison, as well as to their families outside, irrespective of their religious or political background. We wish to show Christian love and friendship to all prisoners, both during and after their detention and release. We support and provide practical care for prisoners' families throughout their separation. Our work is extended through the area by local churches who may refer people to us and vice versa.

Another service we provide is to help newly-released prisoners to find accommodation, friendship and employment where possible in order to enable them to readjust into society.

A great advantage we have over secular organisations set up to help prisoners is that we provide fellowship, Bibles and Christian literature. What's more, we pray for prisoners. As Tennyson once wrote, more good is achieved in this world by prayer than we shall ever know. With the permission of prison authorities and chaplains, we arrange meetings within the prisons for worship and Bible teaching. Indeed, I hope that some of what I have recounted in this book will point out just how much good such meetings can bring about in the lives of prisoners.

Quite apart from me, the list of names of men who have had their lives changed by God could go on and on: Sean, Bobby, Kenny, Packie, Tonto, Liam, Cal, Carol. These are but a few people who went into prison as angry social outcasts, a threat to themselves and others, but who are today shining beacons in a darkened land.

I have plenty of opportunities to go into the schools of Ulster, the breeding grounds for tomorrow's terrorists, some might say. Kids are kids wherever you go in the world, but in Northern Ireland, our kids have to grow up faster than most others in the British Isles.

One particularly poignant incident took place in May of 1991 when I was speaking in a school to a group of fifth-form pupils. I had stood before them, telling them about the events of my life, and how God had come into it to heal my hurts and to redirect my energies into bringing genuine reconciliation to our divided land.

When it was all over, a girl came forward, and with tears welling up in her eyes, she said, 'My father was killed by the IRA. As a member of the Ulster Defence Regiment, he was involved with keeping the peace. He hadn't an enemy in the world. I can't accept that I have to love Catholics after what they did to my dad. And please don't tell me to pray because I'm not a Christian.'

My mind reeled to know what to say. I could see that her hurt was deep. I wanted to hug her and pray for her healing, but it wasn't possible there and then. 'I really believe,' I offered weakly, 'that in time, if you let God into your life, you'll learn to forgive, and by forgiving, your hurts may be healed.'

Her tears were flowing freely now, and her words are as fresh in my ears now as they were then. 'No, I know now that I'll never forgive nor forget.'

Impulsively, I replied, 'God saw what happened to your father. The men who killed him must repent and ask for forgiveness themselves. If they don't, they'll have to answer to God for their crimes. At the end of the day, they'll pay. And I feel sorry for them on that day.'

The girl shook her head and turned away. I don't know if my words sank in, nor indeed do I know if I said the proper thing. But I share this story with you to show you that telling people about Jesus and what he can do in Northern Ireland doesn't automatically solve our problems.

At the end of the day, I have to be satisfied that my work is mainly foundational. I don't know where that girl is today. Nor do I know if she's any closer to being healed of her emotional hurts than she was the day I met her. I can only trust that wherever she is now, she'll remember meeting a former UDA man who learned to love his enemies because of what Jesus Christ did in his life. My prayer is that one day she'll meet another and another, until she finally sees that forgiveness can set her free from the bondage of hate.

To date, one of the most gratifying events of my career with Prison Fellowship occurred on 13th February 1991. That day I stood on a stage with ex-IRA man, Sean Boyle, to talk with students at Belfast's Queens University. Like me, Sean had become a Christian while on remand in Crumlin Road Prison. And, like me, Sean is involved with Christian work. He runs a hostel for homeless people in Derry.

Though Sean was a Republican and I was a Loyalist, and once upon a time our religious and political backgrounds made us deadly enemies, that day we were able to stand united in Christ. Our message before a packed student union could be summed up in one word: reconciliation.

I recall that Sean spoke of integrated education as a way to overcome the differences. 'In this country,' he pointed out, 'the Catholic/Protestant tag is so prominent, whereas in other countries people don't care what religion you are.' He said that politicians in Ulster are too insular. They toe a certain line and are so rigid. That needs to be broken. 'If someone stretches out a hand of peace, then there should be dialogue,' he said.

Sean admitted that his becoming a Christian has opened him up to criticism. Many have accused him of selling out his Republican principles; indeed, of ignoring the lessons of history. 'I've taken a bit of flack in my time, but most people see that I'm genuine,' he pointed out.

Sean was quick to add that Christians aren't the only ones hoping for peace to come to Ireland, but Christians play their part. I agree. For one thing, Christians have a higher allegiance than the State or Crown. We're able to look past flags and slogans. We take our cue from the Prince of Peace. What is more, we are empowered by the Holy Spirit to

> Go into all the world and preach the good news to all creation. Whoever believes and is baptised will be saved, but whoever does not believe will be condemned. And these signs will accompany those who believe: In my name they will drive out demons; they will speak in new tongues; they will pick up snakes with their hands; and when they drink deadly poison, it will not hurt them at all; they will place their hands on sick people, and they will get well (Mark 16:15–18).

I have come to see in my life that the promises made here are real, especially when it comes to spiritual warfare with the unseen powers over our land.

The chance to bring our message of power and forgiveness to the university where tomorrow's leaders meet and exchange ideas was truly an awe-inspiring moment in my life. The response Sean and I got afterwards has convinced me that many people—Catholics as well as Protestants—had their eyes and ears opened for the first time ever that day to the possibility of the power of the cross to heal Ireland.

I don't pretend to be an expert in the politics of Northern Ireland, but this I do know: the situation in my home land is grim, and the political solutions are proving to be futile.

Paradoxically, while the IRA violence is kept in check by virtue of Britain's on-going presence in Northern Ireland, it must be recognised that the presence of British troops on the streets of the Province is deeply resented by thousands of young Roman Catholics, who look on the soldiers as a form of harassment. This resentment leads many of them to join the forces of Irish Republicanism.

Many would disagree with me, but I sincerely believe that if Whitehall were to recall the troops, some of the reasons for young Roman Catholics to engage in terrorism would cease to exist. This in turn would lead to a reduction in support for, and recruitment to, all the paramilitary organisations. The question remains, though, as to how long it would be before one more ugly incident sparked off a reprisal and started another vicious cycle of hatred and fear. After all, this has been the history of Ulster since 1912 and before.

No, I don't accept that political solutions are the way to end Ulster's problems. My own experiences have shown me that the problems in Ulster go beyond the apparent cultural and historical facts. The problem is one of sin and fallen human nature.

If this is so, and I truly believe it is, then the answer to our problems is summed up in the words of a bold banner which hangs from the side of the Metropolitan Church of Belfast, which thousands of motorists may see each day as they commute into the city from the North. The banner proclaims: 'Ulster Still Needs Jesus.' These are not cheap words.

I know I can't change Ulster overnight. But God has led me to my current job working with the men and women in Ulster's prisons. I can tell these people about Jesus and all he longs to do in their lives. The people whom I work with will return one day to society. If I can reach just one other person with the Good News of the gospel, then I will consider my life's work well spent.

# Epilogue

One last word about prisoners. If there is one segment of our society which is branded 'loser' it is people behind bars. Yet Jesus willingly identified himself with prisoners for all time when he said:

> 'Come, you who are blessed by my Father; take your inheritance, the kingdom prepared for you since the creation of the world. For I was hungry and you gave me something to eat, I was thirsty and you gave me something to drink, I was a stranger and you invited me in, I needed clothes and you clothed me, I was sick and you looked after me, I was in prison and you came to visit me.' Then the righteous will answer him, 'Lord, when did we see you hungry and feed you, or thirsty and give you something to drink? When did we see you a stranger and invite you in, or needing clothes and clothe you? When did we see you sick or in prison and go to visit you?' The King will reply, 'I tell you the truth, whatever you did for one of the least of these brothers of mine, you did for me' (Matthew 25:34—40).

Since this is so, I want to end this book with the words of the San Jose Declaration which was drafted in San Jose, Costa Rica on 29th June 1989. It is a manifesto designed to preserve the dignity of prisoners the world over, whatever their religious or political persuasion. The declaration hangs in my office in Belfast and I read it nearly every day:

> We the participants in the Third Triennial Convocation of Prison Fellowship International, hereby declare that:
>
> I. We acknowledge and reaffirm our commitment to the principles stated in the Belfast and Nairobi Declarations (two declarations similar to the San Jose Declaration).
>
> II. We believe that true freedom is found only in and through the Lord Jesus Christ, who breaks the power of sin and sets the prisoner free.
>
> III. We renounce the false freedoms offered by the world, whether through political ideologies, materialism or other philosophies.
>
> IV. We rejoice that Jesus Christ has won for us freedom from the fear and power of Satan and we gratefully witness to the victory of our God over every attack on this Convocation.
>
> V. We confirm our covenant of love and service to prisoners, ex-prisoners and their families in every part of the world, and to each other.
>
> VI. We call upon all governments everywhere to recognize and protect human dignity and the rights of all prisoners to freedom from injustice and oppression.
>
> VII. We condemn the taking of hostages for any reason and call upon the captors of hostages to free them immediately.
>
> VIII. We affirm that freedom from guilt can be found only after confession of sin, repentance and, where possible, restitution.
>
> IX. We recognize that God has chosen to use the weak and powerless to demonstrate His love and mighty power.
>
> X. We pledge ourselves to obey the urgent call of God to extend and deepen our ministry in partnership with

the local church, within the Church universal and in His power alone.

For more information about Prison Fellowship contact:

Prison Fellowship Northern Ireland
39 University Street
Belfast BT7 1FY
Telephone: (Belfast) 243691

Prison Fellowship England & Wales
PO Box 263
London SW1E 6HP
Telephone: 071 582 6221

Prison Fellowship Scotland
PO Box 366
Bishopbriggs
Glasgow G64 2RF
Telephone: 041 762 4887